WARS
AND
THE COMING
APOCALYPSE

DR. MARK A. DUFRENE

WARS AND THE COMING APOCALYPSE
Copyright © 2013 by Dr. Mark A. Dufrene

ISBN: 978-0-9762087-0-9

Contact information for author:

Dr. Mark A. Dufrene
Bayou Connection
www.bayouconnection.com
www.bayouconnection.org

Scripture quotations are New King James unless otherwised noted and quoted from http://www.biblegateway.com

"Scripture taken from the New King James Version®. Copyright © 1982 by Thomas Nelson, Inc. Used by permission. All rights reserved."

THE HOLY BIBLE, NEW INTERNATIONAL VERSION®, NIV® Copyright © 1973, 1978, 1984, 2011 by Biblica, Inc.™ Used by permission. All rights reserved worldwide.

Published by:
Waymaker Publishers
P.O. Box 1481
Fenton, MO 63026
www.waymakerpublishers.com

Cover Design: Keith Cherry and Cass Johnson

Wars
and
The Coming
Apocalypse

Dr. Mark A. Dufrene

ACKNOWLEDGEMENTS

I would like to express my gratitude to the many people who helped me throughout this book project, to all those who provided support, listened to me teach on this subject, read, wrote, offered comments and assisted in the editing, proofreading and design.

My wife Dianna has served in the single most important support role in my life and ministry since we first partnered in teaching a bible study in her home two years before we married. In our 32 years of marriage she has never wavered to wholeheartedly follow the call of God upon our lives having lived in 19 different homes in three different States.

Besides all the ministry-related support she is the mother of my two children, Courtney and Stephanie. She is truly a Godsend to me and the ministry we have been called to.

I have been blessed with a team of editors who made great contributions to the final draft of the book. Dr. Eddy Brown served as a contributing editor and had a profound impact on many thoughts, subjects and certain chapters of the book. Chapters 7 & 8 were written largely due to his prodding. He has been my spiritual father, mentor, scholar and friend for more than 35 years.

His wife Dr. Mary Brown also served as an editor. Like Eddy she has been a great encourager and prayer warrior. While writing the book I became so overwhelmed with a life-threatening illness it was uncertain whether I would live long enough to see the book to completion. Because of the persistent prayers of Dr. Mary Brown and others, the book is complete and I am healed!

Lynda Deniger, a freelance writer and children's author in the New Orleans area, labored many late night hours editing and helping to bring simplicity to some of the very complex subjects within the book. Both she and her husband Ron have been a great source of encouragement and help.

David Wilkins, a retired scientist with the space program, has made a profound impact upon my personal life and the contents of the book. David is a rare find in today's world. Not many with his background even acknowledge the existence of God. His scientific contribution added a dimension to the work in a field of study that is often not considered in Biblical writings.

Cumberland Worship Center, the church I pastor in Crossville, Tennessee has been very supportive of my work. Their continued feedback about the many varied subjects has been extremely helpful as I organized my thoughts for the writing.

My publisher Donna Cherry and her husband Keith who designed the cover have been a great joy to work with. Donna's attention to detail and the presentation of the book is noteworthy, and their encouragement is a Godsend. I would not have wanted to do this without their contribution.

In 1975 I met two pastors who made a tremendous impact upon my life. The preaching ministry of Reverend Marvin Gorman led to my salvation experience and gave me a passion for ministry. His dynamic preaching of the Word of God gave me a hunger to know the God of my salvation and to dedicate my life to the Call of God. Writing this book is an answer to that call.

Several months after my salvation experience I met Reverend Paul Radke, Pastor of the Westwego Assembly of God Church in Westwego, Louisiana. In a Sunday evening church service in the fall 1975, Pastor Radke showed the film "The Road to Armageddon" by David Wilkerson. Realizing the impact the film had on me Pastor Radke invited me to his home after the service to have a hamburger with him and his family. As we sat in his living room, I badgered him with a lifetime of questions. It was there that it all began and from that point life would never be the same. My journey to understand the mysteries of the return of Jesus Christ began with the watching of that film and a conversation that followed in the home of Pastor Radke.

There is neither time nor space to acknowledge all who have helped along this journey. But I want to express my thanks to the many not mentioned.

ABOUT THE AUTHOR

Pastor Mark is from the bayous of South Louisiana where his Cajun, French-speaking family has lived most of their lives. Although raised in the Catholic Church, he had a born again experience in an Assembly of God Church in September 1975.

Shortly after his salvation experience, he felt a strong calling to begin his ministry in the French Quarter of New Orleans. "I learned to communicate the gospel by reaching out to alcoholics, drug addicts and homeless people," says Pastor Mark. "Street evangelism gave me a burden for people and I learned to love the unlovable rejects that lived on the street." He spent several years in street evangelism before attending Christ for the Nations Bible School in Dallas, Texas where he began his studies in Theology.

During the years of street ministry, he and his wife, Dianna, became pastors of an inner city outreach ministry in New Orleans. It was there that God began to prepare them for pastoral ministry and church planting.

In 1982, Mark and Dianna devoted their lives to church planting. Since that time, they have planted four churches, two in Louisiana, a church in Florida and Tennessee. They also helped build several churches in Romania.

Today, Mark and Di are the Senior Pastors of Cumberland Worship Center in Crossville, Tennessee. He serves as a presbyter for the ministerial organization Global Fellowship. He also serves on the Board of Directors for International Gospel Outreach a mission training and sending organization located in Semmes, Alabama.

Pastor Mark is a gifted communicator of the gospel that has learned the art of making things that are very complex simple. He is known best for his creative use of illustrated sermons and also teaching on the subject of Eschatology. He has produced radio broadcast in Louisiana, Tennessee, Florida and Alabama. In 2010 He received an Honorary Doctorate Degree from Mid West Seminary of Bible Theology for his work in Missions and Evangelism.

Aside from the ministry, "Captain Mark" loves joke telling and Cajun humor. He sometimes performs comedy routines for charitable organizations and the elderly in assisted living communities. He loves the culture of his Cajun heritage in Deep South Louisiana. He hopes one day to return to his roots in the bayou's with the message of Eschatological studies he has obtained through his many years of ministry.

Contents

Contents

FOREWORD

Every once in a while, out of a plethora of Christian books, one will surface that is thought provoking, prolific, and so prophetic it will have you scampering for your Bible as you read the pages. This book by Dr. Mark Dufrene is one of those rare finds. It is researched, relevant, realistic and readable whether one is an experienced scholar and theologian or a person that has limited knowledge in the field of Eschatology.

Mark brings fresh understanding and revelational truth to subjects that many have made so complex. There is a current that flows throughout the book that is not dogmatic but is firm in its confidence to quicken the reader to consider, "What if this is true?". This author has a unique ability to nurture the reader and allow them to come to their own conclusions. The chapter he designates to the families who have lost their loved ones in military conflict and past wars is passionate and encouraging to those who have had broken hearts and a multitude of unanswered questions.

One more nugget that I would like the holder of this book to consider is the question, "Where is Mystery Babylon?". While Dr. Dufrene does not lobby the point, he offers a possibility that you do not find in the writings of apocalyptic pundits.

The bottom line is you will not be able to put this book down and when you finish it you will have both answers and questions. Now this comprises what I call a literary journey that will challenge, encourage and inspire you.

Dr. Eddy Brown, President
International College of Bible Theology

INTRODUCTION

My wife Dianna and I pastor a church in the small town of Crossville, Tennessee located on the Cumberland Plateau near the great Appalachian Mountains. Not long ago our church hosted a celebration to welcome home soldiers who were returning from the war in Iraq and Afghanistan. This commemoration for the National Guard in Cumberland County was called the Yellow Ribbon Event. It was a tremendous honor to be among the great heroes of our U.S. military who have been fighting for our freedom in another part of the world. After the two day event, I was more proud than ever to be a citizen of this great country, and to realize that our military is represented by some very special men and women!

As I watched the debriefing of the soldiers at the Yellow Ribbon Event, I began to wonder what it would be like for these men and women returning home to their families and civilian life. For many, life would never be the same. I remembered the soldiers who returned from the Vietnam War in the '70's. A young man at that time, I vividly recall the struggles so many of them had as they tried to resume a life of normalcy after their many experiences at war.

The Sunday following the event I felt a heaviness in my heart.

That morning I shared with our congregation the importance of praying for these families and how we needed to be sensitive to their needs as they assimilated back into our community. Our church continues to pray for these men, women, and their families.

In the following pages it is my desire to give a Biblical explanation for the purpose of these modern day wars. It goes beyond what is seen in the natural. We will not stop with the subject of wars. We will take a prophetic journey into the near and distant future to see what is revealed through biblical study.

WARS AND THE COMING APOCALYPSE

Wars, how we hate them! I have often thought–what a waste! Most of us long for a world where there will be no more war. My friend, I want you to know that such a world is coming! The Bible speaks of a world that is at peace, free of war and the devastating loss of life and the many sorrows that are the consequences of war. However, before we will see such a time, Jesus said one of the signs of His soon coming return would be "Wars and Rumors of Wars".

Some historians say there have been more than 3,000 wars in recorded history. At a military academic lecture it was stated that peace has only existed for about 5% of recorded history.

No period has witnessed the escalation of wars as has the 20th century. The Red Cross has estimated that over 100 million people have been killed in wars since the 20th century began. Up until 1914 war had never been universal, but in both World War I and II, the world was at war.

It was believed that World War II would make the world safe

for democracy, but the world has been anything but safe. Our history books record numerous major wars and hundreds of rebellions and conflicts since that time. Astoundingly, the death toll in conflicts since the end of World War II has now topped 23 million.

The opening of the Berlin Wall in November of 1989 symbolized the end of the Cold War between the superpowers and much of the world thought this would be the beginning of world peace. Instead of the expected peace, more "wars and rumors of wars" raged around our planet.

Every time there is a conflict in the Middle East the media begins to shout "Armageddon" or "World War III". Some say we are already fighting World War III with the constant worldwide war against radical Islamic terrorism. Since the detonation of the atomic bombs on Hiroshima and Nagasaki at the close of World War II, the world lives in fear of an all-out nuclear holocaust. How long will it for take one of these rogue nations to obtain a nuclear bomb? Wars, rumors of wars and the fear of war are before us every day. Jesus said this is a sign of the times. The world is at war! And we will continue to be at war until Jesus returns.

The Apocalypse

In approximately 90 A.D. Jesus appeared to the Apostle John on the Isle of Patmos and revealed to him the Apocalypse, which is the revelation of things that will take place in the future. One of my main purposes in writing this book is to address the wars of the Apocalyptic period. This will no doubt be one of the most interesting, yet sobering studies in this book. As we begin our study, I'd like to share something Jesus taught His disciples 2,000 years ago on the Mount of Olives.

In the gospel of Matthew chapter 24, Jesus began his teaching with a prophecy about the destruction of the temple in Jerusalem. Then the disciples asked Him, *"Tell us, when will these things be… and what will be the sign of Your coming and the end of the age?"* In response to that question, Jesus began to give them one of the great teachings regarding the signs of the times. He said *"…And you will hear of wars and rumors of wars."* Then He said something that I want you to wrap around you like a seat belt in your car because we are going to take a ride on a bumpy and dangerous road, **"… see that you are not troubled: for all these things must come to pass, but the end is not yet."**

The words, **"See that you are not troubled"** are important. It is a command. Jesus is saying, **"There is something you must do when you see these things happening. See that you are not troubled!"** These are profound words of comfort spoken from the Master before He says, **"For all these things must come to pass, but the end is not yet!"** As you read I want you to remember the words of Jesus and do as He has said, do not allow yourself to be troubled by these things. This study is not written to provoke fear, but to give insight as to what is happening in the world around us, and to prepare us for what is coming. We all hate war. God hates war, but wars will continue until the King of Kings and Lord of Lords rules and reigns in all the earth.

Four Wars

The Bible teaches us that three prophetic wars will erupt in the Apocalyptic period or "the last days". And there will be yet a fourth war at the close of the millennial reign of Christ. They are:

1.   The modern day Iraq war

2.   The war of Gog and Magog

3.   Armageddon

4. The last and final conflict in Biblical prophecy, another war with Gog and Magog

WARS AND SIGNS

In Matthew 16:1-4 the Pharisees and Sadducees were asking Jesus for a sign. Jesus rebuked the religious leaders because they did not recognize the signs about the Messiah that had been given by the Prophets in the Old Testament. Today people are also looking for signs that reveal when the world will come to an end.

It seems that this subject has been around for a long time. Scientists are looking everywhere for answers, from the far reaching cosmos to the depths of the ocean. Historians are dissecting every piece of historical literature that can be found trying to find answers in the Hieroglyphics of ancient Egypt, the Mayans, Nostradamus and other ancient civilizations.

The fact that they are looking so intently encourages me. It also testifies that God, by His Spirit, is actively at work in the earth. The reason there is such curiosity on this subject is because God has put within the hearts of men a desire to know what is going to happen to mankind in the future. What is disappointing is that like the Pharisees and Sadducees of Jesus' day, the signs are staring them in the face but they refuse to see them! I can understand that when it comes to the secular world view, not even the Christian church recognizes some of the most profound and convincing signs since the birth of Christ Himself.

The sign I am speaking of is "War". I am not referring to just any war, but the Apocalyptic wars of the last days! There will be many wars but we are going to bring our attention to the major prophetic wars revealed in Eschatological study.

THE RETURN OF CHRIST

As compelling as the study of Prophetic wars are, they are not our only subject of interest. The beginning chapters deal with the wars of the Apocalyptic Age that point to the greatest event of the Prophetic future—"The Return of Christ". Jesus Christ the Son of God is about to return. Chapter 4 introduces that great event and the profound effect it will have on the entire world.

Chapter 5 highlights many other signs of the times that reveal where we are on God's prophetic timetable. Chapter 6 helps us prepare for the unexpected return of the Lord. In chapters 7 and 8 I write about America, the state we are in as a nation and what we can expect as the prophetic future continues to unfold. Chapter 9 is a word about hope. The book closes with an Epilogue and Appendix. The Epilogue presents a systematic theological study about why we should trust Biblical Prophecy above everything else in the world that is attempting to predict the future of our existence. The Appendix explains the prophetic and scientific significance of the blood red moon on the cover of the book.

As you read remember this. This book has been written with the purpose of bringing to the awareness of this generation the soon coming return of Jesus Christ. I have written about subjects that have many and varied views by some of the great scholars and Bible students in present times and throughout the history of the church. Although we may differ on some of the specifics most all believe that Jesus Christ is about to burst from the clouds with a shout and the sound of the trumpet. This book is the sound of an alarm; it is the trumpet of man sounding, trying to get the attention of all who will hear.

I have prayed the prayer of the Apostle Paul in Ephesians 1:16-21 for everyone that will read the message in this book. I encourage all to pray this prayer for yourselves as we begin a journey in the study of God's Word that has the potential to forever change your life and the world in which we live.

> [16] do not cease to give thanks for you, making mention of you in my prayers: [17] that the God of our Lord Jesus Christ, the Father of glory, may give to you the spirit of wisdom and revelation in the knowledge of Him, [18] the eyes of your understanding being enlightened; that you may know what is the hope of His calling, what are the riches of the glory of His inheritance in the saints, [19] and what is the exceeding greatness of His power toward us who believe, according to the working of His mighty power [20] which He worked in Christ when He raised Him from the dead and seated Him at His right hand in the heavenly places, [21] far above all principality and power and might and dominion, and every name that is named, not only in this age but also in that which is to come.

THE FIRST WAR
IRAQ

CHAPTER 1

If you have not read the introduction, please go back and read it before you continue. This will help you understand why I put such strong emphasis on the wars of the Apocalyptic Age.

The war the U.S. and Allied Forces began in Iraq in 2003 is a prophetic war. This war was prophesied over 2,600 years ago by Bible prophets. Many references are made to this war in the Old Testament by the prophets Jeremiah and Isaiah. They wrote extensively about the prophetic future of ancient Babylon which is modern day Bagdad in Iraq.

Bagdad, the current capital city of Iraq, is ancient Babylon in the Bible. I will use the names of Babylon and Bagdad interchangeably throughout this study for they are one and the same prophetically. It is extremely important to understand the history of this ancient city because Babylon is to the devil what the city of Jerusalem is to God. The city of Babylon had its origin as far back as Genesis. The great hunter Nimrod founded ancient Babylon. In Genesis 11:1-9, it is referred to as the tower of Babel, which historically is known to be the first organized rebellion against God.

The origin of cities and nations is important to the understanding of prophetic wars. The subject of 'origin" which is the beginning of something is important to God because God does not forget the origin of things, cities, nations and civilizations.

The famous ancient city of Babylon, mentioned numerous times in the Bible, was built in the same geographical location as the ancient ruins of the tower of Babel. If you were to travel approximately 30 miles south of modern day Bagdad, you would find the ruins of this aged city, Babylon. The ancient Babylonian empire only dominated the Middle East for 70 years from 608 to 538 B.C. The book of Daniel gives an amazing history about the captivity of Israel in Babylon during this time. Because of its relatively short existence, bible students and scholars have had many questions concerning the extensive prophetic writings about this ancient city. Let's look at three of them.

First, why would there be so much biblical history written about this city? **Second**, why so much prophecy about a city that only existed for 70 years? **Third**, why would there be so many prophecies concerning that city which were not fulfilled in the light of Biblical history? The following may help answer these three questions.

Some modern day scholars and avid students of Eschatology, that I know personally, believe in the possibility of a three phase destruction of Babylon.

1. The first being its destruction in 538 B.C. by the Medes and Persians. As is mentioned in Biblical writings.

2. Second, the economic, governmental and military

destruction of Babylon. This is seen in the prophecies of Jeremiah and Isaiah.

3. And last, the conflict that occurs during the Battle of Armageddon.

Therefore, I believe the three phase destruction of Babylon gives answer as to why so much prophecy was given to a city that only existed as a significant power for 70 years.

THE MILITARY DESTRUCTION OF IRAQ

The recent military invasion of Iraq overthrew their government and completely dismantled their military which resulted in an economical collapse of that nation. This represents the prophetic fulfillment of the second phase of the destruction of Babylon. This prophetic war began during the Gulf War of 1991 when U.S. and Allied forces drove Iraq out of Kuwait. Bible scholars called that war "the beginning of the end". It was the beginning of the fulfillment of Jeremiah and Isaiah's prophecies.

Before the Gulf War began, Iraq had the fourth largest military in the world; it was greatly diminished but not completely destroyed during that war. After the war the "Bully of Bagdad" or as some called him "The Butcher of Bagdad", Saddam Hussein, was still in power and aggressively moved toward building his weapons of mass destruction. His intent was to do everything he could to avenge his adversaries: Israel, America, Great Britain and other allied countries that fought in that war.

To date there have been two phases in the military destruction of Babylon: "Desert Storm", the Gulf war of 1991, and "Iraqi Freedom", the war of 2003. Jeremiah and Isaiah outlined much of what this modern day war would do to Babylon, or modern day Bagdad.

A Clearer Picture

For centuries students of Eschatology have applied the prophecies of Babylon given by Jeremiah and Isaiah to the 538 B.C. invasion of ancient Babylon or to the war of Armageddon in the book of Revelation. Through the passing of time, however, we have a clearer picture than that of our forefathers. I believe the revelation of these modern day wars are a fulfillment of Jeremiah and Isaiah's prophecies, and I will explain why I believe this to be true.

We will begin with Jeremiah 50:9, *"For, lo, I will raise and cause to come up against Babylon an assembly of great nations from the north country: and they shall set themselves in array against her; from thence she shall be taken: their arrows shall be as of a mighty expert man; none shall return in vain"* (KJV).

I believe the modern day war in Iraq was the fulfillment to this prophecy for the following reasons:

- The first invasion of Babylon in 538 B.C. by the Medes and Persians was led by King Cyrus. This prophecy does not refer to that first invasion because the Medes and the Persians came from the east not the north. The ancient Medo-Persian Empire was a neighboring country East of Babylon.

- Isaiah described these invading countries as, *"a far country from the end of heaven"* Isaiah 13:5. In Isaiah's day the term "The end of heaven" was used to describe territories across the great oceans of the world that were not discovered yet, not neighboring countries.

- When the Bible uses the word "north" in this

- prophecy or makes reference to the four points of the compass, it is in reference to the city of Jerusalem in Israel.

- Many scholars believe when Jeremiah said "north" he was referring to the northern hemisphere, which speaks of America and the northern European nations that were a part of the invasion in 2003 and the war of 1991. Everything mentioned directionally in the Bible is referenced from the city of Jerusalem.

Jeremiah 50:9 doesn't refer to the final destruction of Babylon in Revelation 18 during the war of Armageddon either. In the war of Armageddon, Babylon is destroyed by God Himself with plague, famine, death and the wrath of a mighty angel. The armies in opposition to the Anti-Christ are a part of the destruction, but God is the "Man of War" in Armageddon. And in Armageddon the war is climaxed by Jesus bursting through the clouds on a white horse followed by the heavenly army.

A very important point in this scripture are the words, *"For, lo, I will raise and cause to come up against Babylon an assembly of great nations"*. The Iraq war was called "George Bush's War" by the liberal media, but George Bush is not God! God claimed responsibility for this war thousands of years ago. God said, *"I will raise and cause to come up against Babylon..."* Just as God moved upon King Cyrus to invade ancient Babylon in 538 B.C. and liberate the Jews being held captive, once again in 2003 God moved upon political leaders to fulfill His prophetic word.

THE APOCALYPTIC AGE BEGINS

The Iraq war marked the beginning of the Apocalyptic Age. It pushed the button on God's prophetic timetable. It connected the ancient world with the present world. It speaks volumes to the Church as to the return of Jesus Christ. This war moved the second hand of God's prophetic time clock one tick closer to midnight. It also tells us that the great God of Heaven is active and present with His people and has everything under control.

To further confirm this present war with Iraq as a prophetic fulfillment of Jeremiah's prophecy, look at the words, *"their arrows shall be as a mighty expert man, none shall return in vain"*. Could it be that Jeremiah's description referred to J-DAMS, laser guided bombs, smart bombs, tomahawk cruise missiles and other modern day weapons that can strike with pinpoint accuracy?

There are other scriptures of interest in Jeremiah 50 and 51, but time and space only permit me to look at a few select verses. I encourage you to further study these two chapters in the book of Jeremiah.

Jeremiah 51:3 says, *"Against her let the archer bend his bow, and lift himself up against her in his armor. Do not spare her young men; utterly destroy all her army"*. Notice the words *"...utterly destroy all her army"*. This was not accomplished in the invasion of 538 B.C. Ancient Babylon was partially burned by the Medes and the Persians during this time but the city continued to exist beyond the first century A.D. Many historical writings were written from Ancient Babylon dating back to 400 A.D. through 100 B.C., including the writings of the Apostle Peter and the Jewish Talmud. These writings and others document the continued existence of Babylon after the invasion of the Medes and the Persians.

> God orchestrated this war and its outcome and it is important that our generation sees this war for what it is, a fulfillment of Bible prophecy.

When the Medes conquered Babylon, it was not about the arrows of a mighty man or weapons of indignation as Jeremiah and Isaiah prophesied. The Medes engineered an ingenious plan. They dug a canal, diverting the Euphrates River which flowed under the city walls into irrigation canals, allowing Cyrus' army to storm the city from the banks of the river. Both Babylonian and Persian records indicate that when the Medo-Persian army approached Babylon, the people, knowing they were defeated, swung open the gates to admit Cyrus' army without resistance. Belshazzar may have been the only one killed according to Daniel 5:30. Babylon's defeat came by way of an ingenious military strategy not by great weapons and an army of mighty men.

This prophecy cannot possibly refer to the destruction of Babylon in Revelation 18 because the emphasis is on the burning of the city not the destruction of her army. Some of the most reputable scholars believe that during the destruction of Mystery Babylon in Revelation 18 the Anti-Christ and his army are invading Jerusalem at the time of the destruction described in that chapter. Therefore, we can conclude that this particular prophecy and many others in Jeremiah 50 and 51 and Isaiah 13 speak of the modern day Iraq war not the war of 538 B.C. or the war of Armageddon in Revelation chapters 16 through 18.

God orchestrated this war and its outcome and it is important that our generation sees this war for what it is, a fulfillment of Bible prophecy. When we read the Biblical account of ancient history, we are amazed by how actively involved God was in the unfolding of these historical events, such as the first invasion of Babylon in 538 B.C. The question must be asked, **"Why is it that we can see God's involvement in events 2,600 years ago but we can't see what He is doing today?" Today all we see is bad politics, angry terrorists and as some would say, warmongers that just can't live in peace.**

The God that is the same yesterday, today, and forever is just as involved in the present day wars and with the nations that fight these wars as He was thousands of years ago. Do not think for a moment that God would sit idly on His throne in heaven while His creation on earth engages in some of the bloodiest battles the world has ever known. When God identified Himself to Moses in the Sinai, He said His name was "I AM, THAT I AM" which means I am present and active with my people. That promise has never changed.

A Tribute to our Veterans

I would like to pause here and speak to some people who are very dear to my heart. I want to comfort those who have been touched by the Iraq war and the war in Afghanistan. Today, because our soldiers have sacrificed their lives in the fulfillment of Bible prophecy, Iraq no longer has a military and Al-Qaida's training camps have been destroyed in Afghanistan.

If I had the opportunity to address our military, I would explain the Divine purpose for the sacrifice they have made in fighting these wars. I wish I could explain to every mother, father, spouse, child, friend and relative that have lost loved ones to battle that they were divinely appointed by God to do what has been done! Not only do I refer to those who have lost their lives, but also to the many who have been physically and mentally disabled from war.

Jeremiah said in 50:9, "...*their arrows shall be as of a mighty expert man...*" (KJV). Notice the word *"Mighty"*. In heaven these soldiers will be numbered with David's **Great Mighty Men** of old who were given supernatural strength and ability from God Himself to conquer the enemies of God (see II Samuel 23:8-12).

Surely freedom has its price and often that price is the life of people we love. Know this, dear friend, your loved one gave his/her life not only for our freedom, but also that the Kingdom of God may come to earth in great power and glory. The King is coming back. Jesus the Son of the living God is about to return. Soldier, you have had your part in the unfolding of this great event. The Lord God of heaven will honor your sacrifice.

My hope and prayer in this writing is that this message will comfort the many families that mourn, not only from the Iraq and Afghan wars but all the wars the U.S. has fought throughout its history. For this reason, the United States has been used by God to set the stage for the final scenes of world history that lead up to the return of Christ. During the 20th century the U.S. became the greatest superpower the world has ever known. This was ordained by God and her rise to greatness was preceded by many wars that cost the lives of many precious people.

Our Vietnam Heroes

Too often I have heard people say of the Vietnam War, "What a waste!" Know this dear friend, "God wastes nothing!" The reason the U.S. was so dominant in the Afghan and Iraq Wars was because of the wars that preceded these wars. The Vietnam War prepared the U.S. for future wars. Our victories in Afghanistan and Iraq are directly connected to the sacrifice of the many soldiers who gave their lives in this Vietnam conflict, a war that didn't seem to make any sense at the time. Who could deny that some of the greatest lessons we learned in warfare were learned in the jungles of Vietnam?

In the last quarter of the 20th century the U.S. gained air dominance over the entire world. This was seen in the Gulf War in 1991, in Afghanistan and Iraq. What the U.S. learned in the air war in Vietnam produced the greatest Air Force in the world. The military might that has been demonstrated in these recent wars evolved from more than three quarters of a century of fighting two World Wars, the Korean War, Vietnam and other military conflicts including the war on drug lords in Central and South America. As I said earlier, "God will not waste anything." Let not the unwise think that our history and the wars we have fought were a waste!

I remember when the Allied forces began assembling troops for the invasion of Iraq, Saddam Hussein shouted from Bagdad, "These Americans will die in this desert and be defeated just like they were in Vietnam." He underestimated what we learned in Vietnam. It was in Vietnam that the US military developed the mental fortitude and commitment that would be necessary to overthrow Iraq, Afghanistan and any other country that threatens our freedom.

Please understand this, Vietnam Vet and other veterans of U.S. wars, you have served in the greatest military the world has ever known because of the bigger plan orchestrated by God Himself. This country, the United States of America, had to rise to power in the End Times so that God could execute His plan at the end of the ages. And you helped make this happen.

> Who could deny that some of the greatest lessons we learned in warfare were learned in the jungles of Vietnam?

SPECIAL OPPS

Another group of heroes that needs to be mentioned is the Special Operation Forces that serve this country and the world in covert operations. They are the Delta Force, Navy Seals, Green Berets, Rangers, Night Stalkers and many more. Perhaps these are some of the greatest heroes of all because much of what they do is not made known to the public. Many of these soldiers will take their testimonies to their graves, never having the privilege of sharing with the rest of the world the covert missions that have saved the lives of thousands or tens of thousands.

One report I found said the U.S. has 58,000 that serve in the United States Special Operations Command, fighting the aggression of worldwide terrorism. We salute you!

I'd like to tell you about a man in our church named Michael. Michael was a helicopter pilot who served with the Delta Force that fought against the drug lords in the early 1980's in South America. On one of their missions his chopper was hit, sending the gun ship down to the ground. Michael suffered a cervical spine injury. Today this man has fusions in his neck that are held together by titanium plates. He lives with chronic pain.

I watch Michael struggle as he has to" suck it up" every day of his life as he works to provide for his family, in spite of the chronic pain in his body. And then there is the inner pain. More than once he has begun to talk about that experience with words like "...Pastor Mark, there were things we had to do in that war..." and then he pauses in silence for a few moments. He goes on to say something like, "I just have to believe that what we did saved the life of some kid!" Michael is just one of the many unknown heroes who fought secret wars that helped make our world a better place.

Veterans, take this to heart. Do not listen to the idealist and the pessimist in their narrow-minded perception of these wars. Their judgment is born from a lack of understanding that can only be attained with an insight of the prophetic writings of Scripture. The events unfolding on the world scene can only make sense when they are cast against the backdrop of the prophetic writings of the

Bible. And it is to this end that I write! May God Bless the U.S.A. and her Great Mighty Men and Women!

WHY DOES GOD WANT TO DESTROY BABYLON?

It is very important that we understand why God is so determined to destroy this city, historically, presently and in the future. In the beginning of this chapter I mentioned the relevance of the origin of civilizations and cities as it pertains to Bible prophecy. Ancient Babylon has been the birthplace for every cultic and occult practice known to the world. Every false religion, including the practice of witchcraft can be traced back to Ancient Babylon. It has been a literal religious symbol of Satan's hatred for God and His covenant people, Israel.

It was no shock in the Gulf War of 1991 that Saddam Hussein fired his scud missiles into Israel trying to draw Israel into that war. Hussein believed it would divide the Allied forces, along with the hope of destroying Israel in the process. This explains the harsh and angry words of God Himself against Babylon. Let us look to Scripture once again.

Jeremiah 50:14 says, *"Put yourself in array against Babylon all around, all you who bend the bow; Shoot at her, spare no arrows,* ***for she has sinned against the Lord."***

The command to shoot and spare no arrows sounds like the description of "Shock and Awe". "Shock and Awe" was the term for the aerial assault against Iraq on March 22, 2003 that began the war, Iraqi Freedom. Notice the words, *"For she has sinned against the Lord."* Her sin goes all the way back to the rebellion at the tower of Babel and the invasion of Jerusalem that began in 605 B.C. Sin, the origin of sin and its offense against God doesn't just fade away with the passing of time (see Exodus 20). God would have to cease to be God if He allowed sin to go unpunished. This is why Jesus had to die on a cross. And know this, every nation in the world, and that includes the United States of America, that has sinned against God will eventually be judged by God. Oh, that the leaders of this great land would only learn from history.

God spoke through the prophet Jeremiah in chapter 50:24-25 and said, "...*You have indeed been trapped, O Babylon...You have been found and also caught because you have contended against the Lord. The Lord has opened His armory, And has brought out the weapons of His indignation; For this is the work of the Lord God of hosts...*", Notice the words, "*His armory...the weapons of His indignation.*"

> God would have to cease to be God if He allowed sin to go unpunished. This is why Jesus had to die on a cross.

Several years ago, while doing ministry in Florida near two air force bases, I was amazed at how many Spirit-filled believers were serving in the U.S. military. A man in my church named Mike worked in the electronic department at Eglin Air Force Base where they developed and tested the guidance systems of the weapons used in Iraq and Afghanistan. I recently learned that a former friend from Bible school had a degree in physics and was one of the design engineers of the weapon systems that were used in the Iraq and Afghanistan war. God said they were "*the weapons of His indignation.*" His Spirit-filled people have contributed to the making of these weapons that have been used to destroy the military might of Iraq. In Exodus 15:3 the Bible says, "*The Lord is a man of war.*"

Isaiah prophesied the destruction of Babylon in Isaiah 13:5, "*They come from a far country, from the end of heaven, the Lord and His weapons of indignation, to destroy the whole land.*" The words "A far country...from the end of heaven" can only make reference to the western world. In Isaiah's day the end of heaven and a far country were across the oceans of the world that were not yet discovered.

Why didn't we see the relevance of these prophesies before now?

When God speaks prophetically, He speaks from timelessness, and He often addresses something from beginning to end. In Revelation 1:8, Jesus addressed Himself as, *"Alpha and Omega, the beginning and the end"*. When these prophecies were given, it was as though God was speaking to Babylon, referring to its entire existence, from the beginning days of the Babylonian Empire to the final destruction of Babylon in Revelation 18, the War of Armageddon.

This is why it is difficult to know the time frame in which the destruction of Babylon will be fulfilled. It is the unfolding of time that helps us put some of these things in chronological order. Some of the prophecy speaks of the invasion of the Medes and Persians while some refers to the present day war and others speak of the final destruction of Babylon during the War of Armageddon.

It's Getting Closer!

Let me use a modern science analogy to explain my point. The closer we get to an object the more we see and understand its detail. The invention of the telescope brought the far distant universe into our living rooms. Before the invention of the telescope, we could see things out there but we could not see them in detail. Because of their distance there was and still are many mysteries we do not understand.

In one sense, the telescope shortens the distance of time and space. Were it not for the telescope it would take a great deal of time to travel to the far distances of the universe to see that which has been brought closer to us by the way of telescopic lenses. This is what the unfolding of time does for Bible prophecy. The passing of time gives clarity to things that have been seen with blurred vision for centuries. This is what Paul was making reference to in I Corinthians 13:12, *We know in part and we prophecy in part, we see through a blurred lens* (author's paraphrase). As time moves forward, the picture gets closer and our vision of what we are trying to see becomes clearer.

This is also true about light; the more light we have the better we can see, "where there is light there is sight". The Bible says, *"God is light, and in Him is no darkness at all"* (I John. 1:5 KJV). The more knowledge we have about God, prophecy and world events the more light we have. This is why our continued study on this subject is so important. As we study and observe world events, we gather more and more light allowing us to see more clearly. This is why Jesus and Paul used the word "Watch" repetitively as they exhorted the church to prepare for the things coming upon the earth.

Here is another example. Jeremiah 50:9 states *"...their arrows shall be as a mighty expert man, none shall return in vain"* (KJV).

> The closer we get to an object the more we see and understand its detail...as time moves forward, the picture gets closer and our vision of what we are trying to see becomes clearer.

A hundred years ago this really didn't make a lot of sense to anyone attempting to interpret this Scripture. Or the interpreter might have thought, "God is going to give some archers extraordinary ability to shoot arrows". Now with the unfolding of time and modern technology we have altogether different thoughts about what God was saying. Because we are nearer than before and have gathered more light, this prophecy is easy to understand. With laser guided bombs and GPS technology, it's simple. *"None shall return in vain"*. In present time our attitude is, "Of course, we will hit our targets. None of our missiles will return in vain; our technology will not fail us".

Some prophecies cannot be understood until the time of their fulfillment. One of the big mistakes Bible students make in the study of prophecy is that they try to see things that are not yet revealed.

The Lord spoke through Jeremiah in Jeremiah 31:15 and said, *"A voice was heard in Ramah, lamentation, and bitter weeping; Rachael weeping for her children refused to be comforted for her children, because they were not"* (KJV).

When Jeremiah wrote this they had no understanding of what the prophetic word meant. However, approximately 580 years later, shortly after the birth of Christ, Herod had the children of Bethlehem put to death. When Matthew witnessed the killing of the children and the weeping of their mothers, he made reference to Jeremiah's prophecy when he wrote, *"[17]Then was fulfilled that which was spoken by Jeremiah the prophet, saying, [18]In Rama was there a voice heard, lamentation, and weeping, and great mourning, Rachel weeping for her children, and would not be comforted, because they are not. (Matthew 2:17-18 KJV)."* Matthew concluded, "This is that!" This is the only way some prophecies will be understood.

WISDOM FROM ABOVE

Remember this: James said in chapter 3:17, *"But the wisdom that is from above is first pure, then peaceable, gentle, willing to yield, full of mercy and good fruits, without partiality and without hypocrisy"*. That which comes from God is not so complex that only a select few can understand it. If you seek understanding with a pure heart, you will find what you are looking for. It will require devotion and sincerity but it can be found!

WHAT REALLY MATTERS!

In our passionate quest to understand the mysteries of prophecy we must not forget what really matters. Jesus and the prophets gave us prophetic signs concerning the latter days that we might recognize them as they reveal to us what time it is on God's prophetic timetable. In I Thessalonians 5:4-5, Paul said, *"But you, brethren, are not in darkness, so that this day should overtake you as a thief"*. God wants His people to know what time it is. He wants us to be prepared for the things that are coming upon the earth. Do you know what time it is? Do you see the signs? The day of His return is closer than we think!

THE SECOND WAR
GOG AND MAGOG

CHAPTER 2

One of the most compelling fulfillments of Bible Prophecy in our day is the buildup of the Gog and Magog War recorded in Ezekiel 38 & 39. Every believer needs to give their undivided attention to the prophetic fulfillment of this war which is about to dawn on the horizon in the Middle East.

THE RUSSIAN AND IRANIAN CRISIS

It is called the war of Gog and Magog or by some the Russian and Iranian crisis. This war will be the single greatest crisis the world has ever known. The development for this war has been more visible in world news over the past decade, but it has been mounting for almost half a century.

Ezekiel prophesied in Ezekiel 38-39 that in the last days there would be an invasion of Israel by Russia, Iran and Arab nations in the Middle East. Many thought the war in Iraq was the beginning of the War of Gog and Magog, but you will soon realize that this is an entirely different prophetic war.

> ¹ *And the word of the Lord came unto me, saying,*
> ² *Son of man, set thy face against Gog, the land of Magog, the chief prince of Meshech and Tubal, and prophesy against him,*
> ³ *And say, Thus saith the Lord God; Behold, I am against thee, O Gog, the chief prince of Meshech and Tubal:*
> Ezekiel 38:1-3 (KJV)

This prophetic word begins in Ezekiel 38:3 with these sobering words, **"Behold, I am against you."** Here God Himself declares what is about to unfold.

WHO IS GOG AND MAGOG?

For centuries scholars have researched biblical and historical writings to identify Gog and Magog and the other ancient names of this prophecy. The identity of these ancient cities in relation to modern day geography is important to this study.

In the days of Ezekiel Gog was king in the land of Magog and was the Chief Ruler over Rosh, Meshech and Tubol. Gog is a word for a ruler or king with the literal meaning of "the man on top". It is a fitting name for a dictator. The word "Chief" means "head," and is the Hebrew word, Rosh. In his ancient Hebrew lexicon, the Hebrew scholar Gesenius, identified Rosh as "the ancient name for Russia."

Magog was a real nation that occupied a territory known to Ezekiel and the Jewish people in the fifth century. Researchers believe that Magog is the territory we know today as Russia and the southern republics of the former Soviet Union which include Kazakhstan, Tajikistan, and Georgia.

Genesis also mentions Meshech and Tubal. Hebrew scholars

believe Meshech is the ancient city we know as Moscow, and in Ezekiel 38:5-6, the prophet adds several other names to the list of the allied nations that will align themselves with Russia in the invasion of Israel. There are a total of eight proper names in Ezekiel 38:1-7 that represent the geographic location of the Gog and Magog invasion of Israel.

1. Magog
2. Meshech
3. Tubal
4. Persia
5. Ethiopia
6. Gomer
7. Togarmah
8. Libya

Scholars have split theological hairs over how these ancient names correspond with current names. There are some varying opinions, but the most consistent one in everything I have read refers to the nations that surround Israel on the far north, east and southern borders. The key nations of interest are Russia, ancient Persia which is modern day Iran, and North African nations.

"Hook in Your Jaw"

Ezekiel 38:4 reads, *"I will turn you around, put hooks into your jaws, and lead you out, with all your army, horses, and horsemen, all splendidly clothed, a great company with bucklers and shields, all of them handling swords".* **Once again, just as in the Iraq war God claims responsibility for initiating this war.**

The words, *"…put hooks in your jaws,"* is a metaphoric statement. To put a hook in the jaw is similar to using a bit and bridle with a horse or mule, although more graphic, painful and bloody. It suggests that something bloody, and of great force and pain, will cause Russia to join hands with Iran and initiate an invasion against Israel. A fisherman knows that when a fish is hooked in the jaw, the fish will fight at first, but eventually it has no choice but to yield to the pulling of the fishing line. Metaphorically, this is Russia.

Russia has not historically been an aggressor in the face of war. In WW II Russia did not get involved until they had no choice. Eventually, they had to defend their land from the invasion of Germany, but they did not eagerly go to war. Russia's involvement in this war will be like the fish with a hook in his mouth. In the beginning she will resist. At the moment Russia doesn't want anything to do with a war against Israel. But the prophetic word says, *"I will turn you around"* and after a period of time and persistent pressure from oil rich Iran, Russia will turn and give in.

As I write this book, there is a serious threat to the beginning of this war. Iran is developing its nuclear capabilities, and at the same time making threats to wipe Israel off the map. The world knows that when Iran develops a nuclear bomb they will use it against Israel. Israel has a short time to make a preemptive strike against Iran to prevent the intended destruction of their land.

Israel has no choice but to dismantle Iran's nuclear capabilities. When Israel makes her move against Iran, the offensive aggression may be that which provokes the fulfillment of the Prophetic metaphor "...hook in your jaw". The assault will be bloody and painful, and it will leave Russia with no other alternative but to align herself with Iran in a war against Israel.

Why Another War?

"Why another war?" I remind you again of the necessity of understanding the "origins" of the civilizations we have already discussed.

God made a promise to Abraham in Genesis 12:3, *"I will bless those who bless you, And I will curse him who curses you"* (KJV).

God does not forget sin or the origin of sin with the passing of time. A Biblical example is found in I Samuel 15:2-3 (KJV) where God instructed Saul, the first King of Israel, to destroy Amalek and stated the reason why.

> ² *Thus saith the Lord of hosts, I remember that which Amalek did to Israel, how he laid wait for him in the way, when he came up from Egypt.*
> ³ *Now go and smite Amalek, and utterly destroy all that they have, and spare them not; but slay both man and woman, infant and suckling, ox and sheep, camel and ass.*

When Moses led Israel out of Egypt, Amalek opposed God and the Israelites in the wilderness (Exodus 17:8-13). Amalek represented all evil power and opposition to God and His people and His truth. Because of this opposition, after hundreds of years had passed, God sent Saul and the army of Israel to destroy Amalek. The lesson here is that if you oppose God's people, it is no different than opposing God Himself.

> The world knows that when Iran develops a nuclear bomb they will use it against Israel...
>
> Israel has no choice but to dismantle Iran's nuclear capabilities

GOD WILL NOT REMAIN SILENT!

God is not passive as some modern day false teachers and false prophets would suggest. I remember when Congress was debating the Iraq war in 2002. One of the most well-known and influential television preachers addressed the war in one of his broadcasts. He said, "This war is not the will of God...we need to pray this war never takes place." He went on to exercise his authority by praying against the war. Several weeks after the war was in progress he said, "The reason this war happened is because the church didn't pray hard enough." Basically, he was implying that it was the Church's fault.

I get concerned about preachers who are so idealistic, and I am especially concerned about the influence they have on the Body of Christ. **The problem, with those who think this way, is that the god they serve is a god they have created in their mind, not the God of the Bible!**

God is holy, He is also just and righteous, we must never forget this about God. The words "just" and "righteousness" in the English language are two different words. In both the Hebrew Old Testament and the Greek New Testament there is only one word group behind these two English terms. Because of these Divine attributes of our creator, He cannot allow sin to go unpunished. If He did He would have to cease to be God. In Hebrews 10:30-31 the writer says, *"For we know Him who said, Vengeance is mine, I will repay, says the Lord. And again, The Lord will judge His people. It is a fearful thing to fall into the hands of the living God"*.

Terrible atrocities have taken place throughout history and continue to this day. Because of the patience and mercy of God, many think evildoers are getting away with the evil deeds they have committed against God and humanity. Bible history and prophecy tell us something different.

It begins with the persecution of God's covenant people, the Jews. The nations that come against Israel in the Gog and Magog war are guilty of persecuting the Jews and other ethnic groups throughout history.

In Old Testament history all the nations God judged were polytheistic, which means they believed in many gods. *"You shall* have no other gods before me" (Exodus 20:3 NKJV). In the Ten Commandments given to Moses, God addressed polytheism, the worship of many gods, not atheism.

King David, however, addressed atheism in Psalm 14:1, "The fool has said in his heart, there is no God". Communist Russia was atheistic; they denied the very existence of God. Although atheism can be dated back to Old Testament times, no nation in the history of man influenced the world with atheism like Soviet Russia. Millions of people are in a devil's hell today because of the Soviet agenda, Atheism.

In the 20th century the world mourned the revelations of Hitler's atrocities during WW II. Forgotten or overlooked were the atrocities of Joseph Stalin. In 1928 Stalin was entrenched as the Supreme Soviet leader.

Under Stalin's dictatorship, tens of millions of ordinary people were executed or imprisoned in labor camps that were little more than death camps. Perceived political orientation was the key variable, but gender was also a role in these mass atrocities as well. Many believe the "Purge Period" of Soviet history is the worst gendercide of the 20th century, exceeding that of Hitler's reign of terror.

God has not forgotten! In Ezekiel 38:3 God says, "Behold, I am against you, O Gog, the prince of Rosh, Meshech, and Tubal." His judgment against these nations is justified by their hatred for God and His people.

THE TIME OF THIS WAR

Ezekiel 38:8 says, "After many days you will be visited. In the latter years you will come into the land of those brought back from the sword and gathered from many people on the mountains of

Israel, which had long been desolate; they were brought out of the nations, and now all of them dwell safely."

In verses 8-12 the time of the invasion is identified. It begins with the words in verse 8, *"In the latter years"* which speaks of now. The next words identify another specific time when He says, *"Into the land of those brought back from the sword ...which had long been desolate; they were brought out of the nations, and now all of them dwell safely."*

In the prophetic word, God first identified the time this would take place as *"...the latter years".* Then He identified the people, Israel, who had been scattered all over the world since 70 A.D. Notice the words, *"...the land of those brought back from the sword."* This speaks of the nearly 2,000 years the Jews were scattered and persecuted all over the world without a home, which refers to national Israel.

The prophecy is directly related to Ezekiel 37, about the regathering of Israel commonly known as the prophecy of *"the valley of dry bones."* I encourage you to study this chapter because it is so closely related to the prophetic words in chapters 38 and 39. The prophecy of the regathering of Israel in chapter 37 had to precede the Gog and Magog War which is revealed in the following chapters 38 and 39.

After being scattered all over the world since 70 A.D., once again Israel became a nation in 1948. This was the fulfillment of Ezekiel 37. However, the prophecy is only partially fulfilled. The regathering has taken place but chapter 37 verse 14 is yet to be fulfilled, which speaks of the spiritual rebirth of Israel. This will not be fulfilled until Israel receives Jesus as their Messiah. This will not happen until the War of Armageddon.

THE CHRONOLOGY OF EVENTS

For the sake of easy reference, and in order to present a clearer picture of the things we have covered thus far, I want to list the timeline of events:

- The destruction of Jerusalem in 70 A.D.

- The scattering of the Jews throughout the world, which caused them to lose their identity and suffer persecution for nearly 2,000 years.

- The regathering of the Jews to National Israel in 1948 following WW II.

- The fulfillment of Jeremiah and Isaiah's prophecies, the Iraq war, Desert Storm 1991 and Iraqi Freedom 2003.

There are two things we have experienced in the past two decades that had to happen before the Gog and Magog War could take place.

1. The Soviet Union had to fall. When the Soviet Union was in power, Communism was the biggest deterrent to war in the Middle East. As long as Communist Russia ruled that northern part of the world, there could never be a strong Islamic influence in that geographic region that could rise up to lead the Gog and Magog War.

When the "Iron Curtain" fell, religious groups from all over the world rushed into Russia, including Islam. Presently, there is a strong Islamic influence in Russia and all of the former Soviet countries. This had to happen for the alliance of the Russian, Iran and the Arab nations to take place. There will be many reasons why Russia will agree to invade Israel, but the Islamic influence will be a major reason why Russia takes part in this war.

2. Saddam Hussein had to be dethroned and Iraq had to fall. As long as Saddam Hussein ruled Iraq, the "Bully of Bagdad" ruled the Arab nations. From 1980 – 1988 there was a war between Iran and Iraq over a border dispute. During this time these nations were so focused on fighting each other, the rest of the world was not threatened by them. After the cease fire in 1988, three years later, Saddam invaded Kuwait. Saddam's aggression was a menace to the Middle East but he also kept Iran under his thumb.

Before Iraq was invaded by the Allied troops we did not hear very much about Iran. However, now that Iraq is out of the picture, Iran has become the "Big Bully" in the Middle East. Mahmoud Ahmadinejad repeatedly makes threats to wipe Israel off the face of the earth, which leads us back to the prophetic word in Ezekiel 38:10-12. Read this Scripture very carefully because this is what is going on in the minds of both Iranian and Russian leaders. It reveals that there is another entity behind these events. We know this to be our adversary, the devil, who can plant his evil thoughts in the minds and hearts of men.

> [10] *"Thus says the Lord God: On that day it shall come to pass that thoughts will arise in your mind, and you will make an evil plan:*
> [11] *You will say I will go up against a land of unwalled villages; I will go to a peaceful people, who dwell safely, all of them dwelling without walls, and having neither bars nor gates.*
> [12] *To take plunder and to take booty, to stretch out your hand against the waste places that are again inhabited, and against a people gathered from the nations..."*

It is as though Ezekiel could see our day and the daily news headlines from around the world. There are two irrefutable things in these Scriptures:

1. Without a doubt Iran is the one the Lord addresses as having an evil thought arising in their mind. Mahmoud Ahmadinejad and Iran will be strongly driven by the Islamic agenda to destroy Israel. Russia's agenda will be somewhat different. It is better understood in verse 12 motivated by the monetary gain of conquering the land. Its desperate need of financial gain and the supply of oil from these Muslim Nations may also serve as the "Hook in the Jaw" that draws Russia into the war.

> Now that Iraq is out of the picture, Iran has become the "Big Bully" in the Middle East.

2. The people and nation mentioned here is Israel "...*a land of unwalled villages...a peaceful people, who dwell safely...against a people gathered from the nations.*" This can only make reference to Israel.

As you read this book, this war is on the horizon. One would have to be blind not to realize what is taking place in the Middle East with Russia, Iran and their threat to Israel.

WHEN WILL THIS WAR TAKE PLACE?

The question at hand is: Will this war take place *before* the Rapture of the Church or *after* the Rapture of the Church? (Chapter 4 gives a detailed description of the Rapture of the Church.) According to Scripture there is no absolute answer to this question. Of the many scholars I revere on this subject, some believe it will take place almost immediately following the Rapture.

There are a few who believe it could take place before the Rapture. I do not believe we can be dogmatic on either position. Nothing written prophetically gives an absolute answer to this question.

Let's look at some of the possibilities revealed in scripture. In Ezekiel 38:13 we have what many feel is a disturbing revelation of the attitude of the western nations when this invasion comes against Israel. These ancient names used in this Scripture make reference to Western Europe, Great Britain and the United States.

> [13] *"Sheba, Dedan, the merchants of Tarshish, and all their young lions will say to you, Have you come to take plunder? Have you gathered your army to take booty, to carry away silver and gold, to take away livestock and goods, to take great plunder?"*

This totally passive attitude acknowledges what is happening with no incentive to do anything about it. The real question is: Why has the West become so passive about an aggression of this magnitude against its ally Israel when the U.S. has stood with her for so many years? What has precipitated this change of heart?

Futuristic Possibilities

Let us consider a few possibilities:

1. The Rapture has already taken place, producing a chain of chaotic events that cause these countries to neither have the will or resources to act upon. And, if only 10% (approximately 30 million) of Americans go up in the Rapture, it will cause a threefold collapse in the U.S., first in the Economy, second in the Military, and thirdly in the Government. The same will hold true for Western Europe and other nations of the world. However, the Islamic nations will not be as severely impacted.

2. At this time in the future the West has abandoned Israel. Administrative changes in the U.S. in 2008 brought about an entirely different posture regarding the Middle East and Israel. And this is unfolding before us daily with Washington's agenda to downsize our military.

3. Could the West's pre-Rapture attitude symbolize such an economic collapse that they simply can't do anything about it? Even if the desire is there to help, they are helpless because there is neither the money nor the military capable of responding.

These thoughts are sobering, and that is exactly what the revelation of these things should be. In light of all these things that are coming upon the earth, Paul said in I Thessalonians 5:6, *"Therefore let us not sleep as others do, but let us watch and be sober."*

My greatest burden in this situation is that I truly believe God's people are sleeping. We have heard about the return of Christ for so many years that it no longer impacts the average Christian. This is the message of the "Ten Virgins" in Matthew 25 (which I will expound upon in Chapter 6). The Church of Jesus Christ is simply not ready for what is about to take place.

A Cataclysmic Ending

I'd like to mention three more significant points in my final words on this prophetic war. **First,** what will happen to Israel when these nations launch the Gog and Magog invasion? **Second,** what will God do? **Third**, what will be the end result?

I. WHAT WILL HAPPEN TO ISRAEL?

Israel will have a visitation from the God of their fathers as

God Himself intervenes on their behalf. It is the intervention of "Jehovah" God who distinguishes this war from Armageddon. In Armageddon it is Jesus who intervenes. In this war it is Jehovah the supreme God of the Hebrews who intervenes on behalf of Israel.

Israel will learn that the western nations that have helped balance the affairs of the Middle East since the regathering in 1948 are not her God! America, Great Britain and others who have stood by her for more than half a century are not Israel's Savior. This war will result in the "Lord God Jehovah" being hallowed before their eyes (Ezekiel 38:16).

II. WHAT WILL GOD DO?

God is going to reveal attributes about Himself to Israel and to the world that have not been seen since the ten plagues came over Egypt during the Exodus. For thousands of years God, in His patience and mercy, has withheld His judgment and wrath giving man every opportunity imaginable to

> Israel will have a visitation from the God of their fathers as...Jehovah God ..the supreme God of the Hebrews intervenes on behalf of Israel.

turn from his wicked ways and receive His Son as his Savior. But man has hardened his heart and resisted the Goodness of God. Therefore, God will release His fury upon these nations that come against Israel, "...My fury will show in My face. For in My jealousy and in the fire of My wrath I have spoken:" (Ezekiel 38:18-19).

It is outlined in great detail in Ezekiel 38:18-22.

1. There will be an earthquake of such magnitude that the Richter scales of modern times will not be able to measure the seismic activity. Tsunamis will race across

the oceans of the world causing devastation never before seen by man. It will be so devastating that it will affect the fish of the sea, the birds of the air, the beasts of the field and even the reptiles and insects. All men on the earth will feel the devastation. It will change the landscape of the Middle East and beyond as the mountains move from their places and cliffs of rocks fall to the ground and demolish everything around them.

> [19]"...'Surely in that day there shall be a great earthquake in the land of Israel, [20] so that the fish of the sea, the birds of heavens, the beasts of the field, all creeping things that creep on the earth, and all men who are on the face of the earth shall shake at My presence. The mountains shall be thrown down; the steep places shall fall to the ground.'
>
> Ezekiel 38:19-20

2. There will be mass confusion among these warring nations that have come together to destroy Israel. As in the days of Gideon (Judges 7:20-22), God will cause confusion among them and they will turn against one another. This is not hard to believe because these people live in a state of mass confusion. They are already fighting against one another and killing one another!

> [21]I will call for a sword against Gog throughout all my mountains...Every man's sword will be against his brother.
>
> Ezekiel 38:21

3. The death and suffering will be so massive that disease and plague will break out among the armies of Gog and Magog.

> ^{22}"And I will bring him to judgment with pestilence and bloodshed;
>
> Ezekiel 38:22a

4. After all that, there will be flooding rain. We have recently seen what heavy rains can do to mountainous areas as tropical storms move across Central and North America. They cause massive landslides and mudslides that destroy everything in their paths.

> ^{22}...I will rain down on him, on his troops, and on many peoples who are with him, flooding rain...
>
> Ezekiel 38:22b

5. Then fire will fall from heaven. I am reminded of fire falling from the sky and setting ablaze the entire countryside of Egypt during the Exodus led by Moses. And also the fire and brimstone that destroyed Sodom and Gomorrah.

> ^{22}...great hailstones, fire, and brimstone.
>
> Ezekiel 38:22c

III. THE END RESULT

There is something of great eternal value that will take place in the midst of all this cataclysmic destruction. Once again we look to Scripture.

> ^{16}"...so that the nations may know Me."

> ^{23}"...I will be known in the eyes of many nations. Then they shall know that I am the Lord."
>
> Ezekiel 38:16, 23 and,

> ^{6}"...Then they shall know that I am the Lord."
>
> Ezekiel 39:6

Through this outpouring of God's wrath as He intervenes on behalf of Israel, there will be a revelation of God to the nations. It does not lead to the salvation of National Israel, but it will cause some level of spiritual awakening to Israel and the world.

END-TIME REVIVAL?

Does this catastrophic event lead to an End-Time Revival? For decades I have heard many preach and teach that there will be a revival in the End-Times. Will this be that which sparks a world-wide spiritual awakening that many are waiting for? I would say that possibility always exists, but I would not attempt to build a doctrine for an End-Time Awakening based solely on this Prophetic word given by Ezekiel.

There is no teaching to be found in the study of Systematic Theology that promises a revival in the End-Times. Paul said with no uncertainty that there will be a falling away (Apostasy) leading up to the return of Christ (II Thessalonians 2:3). When Jesus gave the parable of the 10 virgins He suggested a large percentage of the **"active church"** will not be prepared for His return (Matthew 25:1-13).

Some have said, "Hardship and tribulation, war, natural disasters, etcetera, will cause people to turn to God". That is simply not true. If it were true the world would already be in a revival because there is great and devastating hardship worldwide as I write. Difficulties have more often than not caused people to harden their heart towards God just as the Bible says Pharaoh did in the days of Moses.

Others have said there has to be a spiritual awakening before the return of Christ because the church needs to be cleansed. They claim the church is not *"Without, spot, wrinkle…or blemish"* and suggest difficulty, hardship and a revival will cause this to happen. I would say to you that it is the blood of Christ that cleanses us and prepares us to meet Him. There is no spiritual exercise one can submit himself to that can possibly cause you to be spiritually cleansed beyond that of the shed blood of our Savior. If there were, Jesus would not have had to die on a cross!

In my lifetime I have watched people become hard and indifferent to world shaking events. In the fall of 1990 the U.S. and allied forces were assembling in the Middle East for Operation Desert Shield. Fear gripped the world as many thought this was the beginning of Armageddon. According to one survey leading up to the war, which was given the name "Desert Storm" and began on January 17, 1991, church attendance had increased by 38%. Fearing Armageddon or WW III people quickly ran to church and called out to God for fear of that which threatened the entire world. Twelve months later the survey was taken again in the same churches that were surveyed before and showed a 45% decrease.

> Some have said, "Hardship and tribulation, war, natural disasters, etcetera, will cause people to turn to God". That is simply not true. People have become hard and indifferent to world shaking events.

In 2001 there was "911", once again people ran to church, but this time their spiritual motivation only lasted about two weeks. Several weeks later everything was back to normal.

In 2007 – 2008 the global financial crisis spread across America like wild fire. This time the reaction was all together different. There was no measurable increase in church attendance, many churches showed a decline during this most difficult time in world history.

And today we are experiencing the worst decline in the Christian Church in American history.

People have become numb to much of what is happening on a global scale. The fear of God no longer has a place in the ideology of our modern culture. People do not run to God or fear God today. People run to the government to have their needs met and the only fear they have is the political agenda that threatens to take away their entitlements.

However, having said all that, according to the prophetic word given by Ezekiel this Gog and Magog war will have a profound impact upon the world. Some will be spiritually awakened by the devastating things that will unfold and call upon the Lord. The question to all is this: **"Why is it that devastation and pain are the only language some will ever understand?"**

ARMAGEDDON AND THE FINAL CONFLICT

CHAPTER 3

Armageddon has become one of the most commonly used terms in reference to war and the feared Apocalypse of the near future. It is everywhere–science, news media, motion pictures and magazines. It is synonymous with the end of the world, but only the world as we know it today.

Before I began this chapter, I gave careful thought as to what I wanted to say about Armageddon. I am not interested in describing it as a gruesome blood bath, but I do want to provide you with an understanding of the events, key cities, nations, people and timeline.

Armageddon is the most difficult war to write about. I believe this is true because the Bible is written to God's covenant people, not the world. Contained within the Bible is a message for the entire world but the Scriptures are written to the Believer. The Believer doesn't have a need to know much about the details of the War of Armageddon because we will be with Jesus in heaven as the war begins to unfold.

I will use what is written to create a word picture in order to give you an understanding about the war. However, the picture is vague; we do not see this war with the clarity revealed in the first two wars of the Apocalyptic Age. We simply do not have the details. It is my opinion that most of what has been written by others embraces far too much speculation. Therefore, if what I have written lacks the clarity of the first two wars we have covered, it may be because that is the way the Lord meant for it to be.

ARMAGEDDON

Armageddon is the last great war of the Apocalyptic period. The term Armageddon comes from the Hebrew language. The word used in the Greek New Testament is Harmagedon; Har is the word for "mountain" or "hill". Mageddon is believed to be the ruins of the ancient city Megiddo that overlooks the Valley of Esdraelon located in north central Palestine. Thus, the name itself describes the primary place of the great battle where the armies of the world will meet for the War of all Wars. This war will be centered on two key cities and two key figures.

- **Key Cities:** Jerusalem and Mystery Babylon
- **Key Figures:** Jesus Christ and the Anti-Christ
- **Timeline:** Iraq War, Rapture of the Church, War of Gog and Magog, The Great Tribulation, Armageddon
- **Nations involved in the war:** All the nations of the earth

The first place the word Armageddon is mentioned in the Bible is in Revelation 16:16 where the bowl judgments of the wrath of God are poured out upon the earth by the seven angels. As the sixth bowl (or vial) is being poured out, something happens that sets the stage for the war to begin. In verse 12 it says, *"And the sixth angel poured out his vial upon the great river Euphrates; and the water thereof was dried up, that the way of the kings of the East might be prepared."* Then the scripture gives insight as to the demonic influence that is behind what is happening (Verses 13-14), which also reveals the level to which world leaders have yielded themselves to the influence of demonic spirits.

> *¹⁴ For they are the spirits of devils, working miracles, which go forth unto the kings of the earth and of the whole world, to gather them to the battle of that great day of God Almighty.*
>
> *¹⁵ Behold, I come as a thief. Blessed is he that watcheth, and keepeth his garments, lest he walk naked, and they see his shame.*
>
> *¹⁶ And he gathered them together into a place called in the Hebrew tongue Armageddon.*
>
> Revelation 16:14-16 (KJV)

"...HE GATHERED THEM"

In verse 16 the scripture says something that is synonymous with the two previous wars, the Iraqi war and the war of Gog and Magog, *"And He gathered them together into a place called in the Hebrew tongue Armageddon."* Notice the words, *"...He gathered them."* **For the third time in these apocalyptic wars you see God gathering the armies of the earth for war.**

In verse 17 are some of the most powerful words you will read in the Bible *"...and there came a great voice out of the temple of heaven, from the throne, saying, It is done"* (KJV). The words, *"It is done"* are enough to make you shake. In fact, that is exactly what happens. At the sound of these words there is the greatest earthquake the world has ever known. The great city was divided into three parts. Every island vanished, the mountains were leveled and great hail from heaven fell upon the people of the earth (Revelation 16:17-21).

At the end of the Great Tribulation, there is an outpouring of the wrath of God upon the earth. Then, at the same time of the outpouring of God's wrath He calls the armies of the earth to the Middle East for the final war, Armageddon. The earthly reason they come for the battle is twofold. First, some of the nations come to war against the Anti-Christ. Second, others will come to rid the world of the Jews for they believe the Jews are responsible for all the cataclysmic things happening on the earth during the Great Tribulation.

MYSTERY BABYLON

In Revelation 17:5 there is a descriptive word given to Babylon that has not been used in all the prophetic writings about this city until now, the word "Mystery."

5 And on her forehead a name was written:

MYSTERY, BABYLON THE GREAT, THE MOTHER OF HARLOTS AND OF THE ABOMINATIONS OF THE EARTH.

Identifying this city has been a great mystery to Bible scholars for centuries. I will devote a considerable amount of time to this "Mystery City" for the following reasons:

1. A "Mystery" is something that has been hidden and in reference to this city it has been hidden for 2,000 years.

2. The identity of this city has a connection to the world leader in the end time, the Anti-Christ.

3. The Mystery City is the primary focus in the Apocalypse leading up to the return of Christ, the biggest word picture in the War of Armageddon.

4. If the Mystery City is revealed in our present time, it will be one of the most significant revelations of the apocalyptic age.

5. The revelation of this city puts us closer to the return of Christ than perhaps any other fulfillment of prophecy in scripture.

As we attempt to solve the "Mystery", we must have an understanding of the Anti-Christ because the destruction of the Anti-Christ is the primary focus of Armageddon. The person of the Anti-Christ and his mission during the Tribulation are directly connected to the Mystery City.

The Anti-Christ

"In the beginning," that is the beginning of the Great Tribulation Period; the world is in shock because of the rapture of the church. Economies have collapsed worldwide, so have governments and their military forces. Anarchy is rampant; the whole world is in utter chaos. The war of Gog and Magog is now history and devastation is everywhere. The world is crying for peace and looking for a leader. The Anti-Christ appears on the world scene. He has a charisma unequal to any man that has ever lived; he is stunning and he is a genius. In fact, he is a genius in every dimension imaginable.

The prophet Daniel described him as an oratorical genius, an intellectual genius, a political genius, a military genius and a commercial genius (Daniel 7:20 - 11:21). Paul described him as a religious genius (II Thessalonians 2:4) and John the revelator describes him as an administrative genius (Revelation 13:1-2).

The Anti-Christ effectively deceives a desperate world with his extraordinary abilities and for the first three and a half years brings a measurable amount of peace to a chaotic world. He leads the world in three dimensions: 1. Politically, 2. Economically, 3. Religiously. If you are familiar with world events you can see the platform being assembled for all three of these major roles as a world leader. For decades political leaders have been calling out for a "New World Order." This New World Order is what the governments of the world are leading us to at this present time. The New World Order is the platform for a One World Leader, the Anti-Christ!

FORERUNNERS OF THE ANTI-CHRIST

In 2008, right before the presidential election the Lord spoke a word to me about a global political agenda orchestrated by the devil himself to prepare the platform for the Anti-Christ. The Spirit of God said to me, **"There are 12 key political leaders worldwide that are being used like a Marionette to prepare the world for the rule of the Anti-Christ"** and "Barak Hussein Obama is one of them." In the Bible 12 is a perfect number, signifying perfection of government or governmental perfection. It is found as a multiple in all that has to do with rule.

Don't take offense to that statement if you are a supporter of President Obama. Almost every president of the U.S. in the past three decades or more has had some role in building this platform and the next president will make his contribution. Not only the president, but U.S. lawmakers are preparing the way for the Anti-Christ by way of their Anti-Christ motivated political agendas.

When Jesus began His ministry, John the Baptist went before Him preparing the way of the Lord by preaching the message of repentance. John is called the forerunner of Jesus Christ. What John the Baptist did for Jesus, political leaders are doing for the Anti-Christ. They are preparing the way for his debut; they are his forerunners. And there are many!

The primary way they are contributing to this is in the increase of bigger government. As the end draws near the governments of the world will continue to get bigger and the global agenda will be to become unified just as the European Union did following World War II. As anyone can see, the end they are working toward is a one world government. This is how the Anti-Christ will rule the world. Making this happen is a long process that involves many decades of time and many worldwide leaders.

> What John the Baptist did for Jesus, political leaders are doing for the Anti-Christ. They are preparing the way for his debut; they are his forerunners.

The Anti-Christ will rule the world from a city in the Middle East that the Bible calls "Mystery Babylon." The question is: "Where is this city and does it exist today?" Does the historical pattern of **"Modern day Bagdad – Ancient Babylon"** follow through to this point in the Apocalyptic age or does it refer to a different city? To get to the point, I do not believe Mystery Babylon in Revelation 18 is modern day Bagdad and I will give you the reasons why.

There has been much speculation about this city throughout the 20th century. Some have suggested that it could be New York City. Others have believed it would be a new city, one that would be built in the last days, somewhere along the Euphrates River. While still in rule over Iraq, Saddam Husain was rebuilding the walls of Babylon over the ruins of the ancient city up until the day he was dethroned during the war, Iraqi Freedom. Saddam repeatedly compared himself to King Nebuchadnezzar and his life's goal was to recreate the ancient Babylonian Empire in all its glory. This will never happen; God has already dissolved this attempt.

The characteristics of Mystery Babylon revealed in the book of Revelation (Revelation 17 and 18) will help identify what city in the Middle East possibly fits that description. Here is a list of the obvious characteristics:

- The geographical boundary would be limited to the west side of the Euphrates River which eliminates Bagdad or the ruins of ancient Babylon (Revelation 16:12).

- She is a city where all people of every nation reside (Revelation 17:15).

- It will be a city in the Arab world where every religion of the world can be practiced openly (Revelation 18:4).

- Her culture will be sinful and oppressive to the poor (Revelation 18:5).

- The city will have an arrogant attitude about herself (Revelation 18:7).

- The kings and great leaders of the earth will have an investment in her (Revelation 18:9).

- She will be the center of world commerce (Revelation 18:11-17).

- Her appearance will be pure opulence. Gold, silver, exotic woods and fine linen will be everywhere (Revelation 18:12-16).

- She will be known uniquely worldwide for her pearls, precious stones and jewelry industry. Also precious metals, marble and ivory (Revelation 18:12).

- She will be known worldwide as the city that has made men rich (Revelation 18:15).

- She will be a port city with merchants from all over the world (Revelation 18:17). This also eliminates Bagdad and also the possibility of a new city being built on the Euphrates River.

- She will have more wealth than the mind can imagine and men will lust after her wealth (Revelation 18:12-14).

- She will have embraced the defiant attitude of the people of the Tower of Babel (Genesis 11:1-9) and the Ancient Babylonian Empire (Book of Daniel).

- She will be the seat of the Anti-Christ at the end of the Great Tribulation Period.

DUBAI?

There is only one city in the Middle East that has all these characteristics, that city is Dubai. I will share with you why I believe Dubai could be Mystery Babylon and how this idea came to me.

In less than 30 years Dubai has developed from a sleepy little coastal city on the southwest side of the Persian Gulf into the single greatest and most opulent achievement of man in world history. Truly, there has never been anything to compare to her in the entire world.

Historically she was a fishing village known for harvesting some of the largest and most beautiful pearls in the world. Other than her pearls she was mostly insignificant until 1966 when oil was discovered. That changed everything. After the discovery of oil, traders came from all over the world to settle in Dubai which in turn enhanced economic growth at an exponential rate. To describe Dubai in one word, "Opulent" like opulent on steroids!

The city is located in a desert that has an average temperature of 120 degrees. But that didn't deter the vision of the Sheikhs that desire to make the biggest and greatest of everything that exists on the planet. I will highlight some of her achievements:

- The world's tallest buildings, made of the highest quality of everything on the planet, which is the spirit of the Tower of Babel.

- The world's richest horse races.

- The world's tallest and most opulent hotel.

- It is said in Dubai, if it looks like gold it is!

- They are building a theme park twice the size of Disney World.

- There is an indoor snow skiing mountain and lift in the 120 degree desert.

- There are horse stables that look like 5-star hotels.

- They have created their own man-made islands, one which is in the shape of a palm tree. Palm trees grew atop the hanging gardens of ancient Babylon.

- They are also creating islands in the shape of continents.

- There are hundreds of jewelry stores; one visitor said she saw a 52 karat diamond ring and pearl necklaces that measured 15-21mm.

- There are extravagant palaces, hotels and buildings of every kind imaginable.

- She is a port city and is becoming the center of merchant trade from all over the world.

- Time and space do not permit me to list all the extravagant achievements that have shaped Dubai in less than 30 years.

Dubai is synonymous with humongous as it continues to build the first, largest and biggest constructions in the world. She is in constant competition with herself with the urge to construct something bigger and better than the previous structure. In fact, building structures seem to be her obsession. This is reflective in the Burj Khalifa, which is the tallest man-made structure in the world. The skyscraper is 2,723 feet tall—one thousand feet taller than any other building on earth. It cost $1.5 billion to build, and the entire downtown development, where the building sits, cost a staggering $20 billion US dollars.

> In less than 30 years Dubai has developed from a sleepy little coastal city on the southwest side of the Persian Gulf...
>
> To... "Opulent"—like opulent on steroids!

Something of prophetic significance happened during the development of this project that possibly connects Dubai to Mystery Babylon. In Revelation 18:9-10 (NIV) the Bible says when the Mystery City burns during Armageddon the *"Kings of the earth... weep and mourn"*.

The global financial crisis of 2007-2010 led to high vacancies and foreclosures in Dubai. With Dubai mired in debt from its huge ambitions, the government was forced to seek multibillion dollar bailouts from its oil-rich neighbors. This means, the kings of the earth have a great investment in Dubai. This would explain why the kings of the earth will mourn when she burns.

> *"The kings of the earth who committed fornication and lived luxuriously with her will weep and lament for her, when they see the smoke of her burning."*
> Revelation 18:9, 10

This was one of four thoughts that drew my attention to Dubai while researching the characteristics of Mystery Babylon as revealed in the Bible. I observed the four following insights:

1. I could not imagine why the powerful and wealthy from other nations would mourn over a burning city anywhere in the Middle East, except Dubai.

2. She was a major port city catering to merchants from all over the world. None of the traditional cities in any Arab country have that description.

3. The mention of Pearls. At one time I had done research about the history of Dubai and remembered that she was known for harvesting pearls.

4. And then there was the word "mystery". I had studied this word extensively in Biblical studies and believed that it would somehow lead to the possible discovery of this "mystery city."

A mystery is defined as something that is hidden or a secret. The Bible speaks often of secrets and mysteries. In Ephesians 3:3 Paul said, *"...by revelation he made known to me the mystery."* In Daniel 2:28, Daniel said to King Nebuchadnezzar, *"...there is a*

God in heaven that reveals secrets." Yet still another, in Amos 3:7 the scripture says, *"Surely the Lord God does nothing, unless He reveals His secret to His servants the prophets."*

The mysteries and secrets of the Bible are revealed in the time frame of God's choosing. Throughout history God has hidden great truths about man and his future and will not reveal them until the appointed time. As an example: The mystery of the church age was not revealed until after the life and ministry of Christ by the writings of the Apostles, primarily Paul. The prophets of the Old Testament did not see or understand the existence of the Church or its ministry following the life of the Messiah.

Therefore, if God allows this mystery that has been hidden for 2,000 years to be revealed to the Church now, the revelation is very significant to understanding how close we really are to the final stages of the Apocalypse.

The Anti-Christ will rule the world Politically, Economically and Religiously. Dubai is the only city in the Middle East where he can do all three. Dubai has an ecumenical approach to the practice of religion. She is predominately a Muslim nation with more than 80 percent Muslims. However, she permits the practice of religions from all over the world. There are several Buddhist temples and Christian churches in Dubai. No other Arab country in the world would permit such religious tolerance!

Dubai fulfills all the characteristics of the Biblical meaning of mystery. The city has been hidden in the deserts of the Middle East nearly unheard of for 2,000 years. Few people have known much about the greatness of Dubai well into the 21st century. The city is still veiled from much of the known world.

I do not believe it is wise to be dogmatic about drawing final conclusions about things that are identified as a mystery. For the reasons stated above we can easily see the many possibilities why Dubai could be that city, but there is always the "What if..."! I think it is wise to leave it with a "?". Only time will tell if Dubai is this mystery city of Revelation. When the time comes for the mystery to be solved beyond question or doubt we, the Church, will no longer be here. We will be with Jesus waiting for His grand descent on a white horse when we burst through the sky with Him to bring an end to Armageddon.

The Final Battle

At the end of the Great Tribulation Period the Anti-Christ will rule the world from the Mystery City. Many believe his rule begins in Europe but is possibly forced out of Europe midway through the Tribulation because of what Jesus called, *"The Abomination of Desolation",* spoken of by Daniel the prophet (Matthew 24:15). This is when the Anti-Christ enters the temple in Jerusalem and proclaims himself to be God. This divides the world. Some will remain loyal to him and others will become his enemy.

This explains why Revelation 18 details the burning of the Mystery City, leading up to the Second Coming of Christ on a white horse in Revelation 19:11. However, it is not Jesus' coming that brings about the burning of the Mystery City. God has moved upon other nations of the world to war against the Anti-Christ and it appears their assault begins with an attack against the Mystery City.

> I do not believe it is wise to be dogmatic about drawing final conclusions about things that are identified as a mystery.

How long will Armageddon be in progress before Jesus appears is unknown. It could be months, weeks or just a few days.

There is no definitive answer. I will list some of the significant facts that are clearly revealed in scripture about the war.

1. Kings of the whole earth are gathered to the Middle East for the great battle.

> *"For they are spirits of demons, performing signs, which go out to the kings of the earth and of the whole world, to gather them to the battle of the great day of God Almighty"*
>
> Revelation 16:14

2. The aggression by world leaders to come to the Middle East for war is motivated by three demonic, unclean spirits like frogs (Revelation 16:13). The three spirits are described as follows:

   ▸ The dragon – Satan

   ▸ The beast – Anti-Christ

   ▸ The false prophet

> [13]*"And I saw three unclean spirits like frogs coming out of the mouth of the dragon, out of the mouth of the beast, and out of the mouth of the false prophet."*
>
> Revelation 16:13

Scripture says that the powers of these spirits are manifest by way of what comes out of their mouth. The world is deceived by the seductive words spoken by the deceivers. Don't underestimate the power of the words the deceiver uses to control the whole world.

3. There is also the working of miracles going forth to the kings of the earth to gather them to battle.

"For they are spirits of demons performing signs"
Revelation 16:14

This is an interesting insight to man's vulnerability to the manifestations of miracles. Our world hungers for the manifestation of miracles, and the Anti-Christ will satisfy that hunger with all the miracles that one can imagine. We must be cautious, just because it is miraculous does not mean it is of God! (read Matthew 7:15-23)

4. The Anti-Christ will war against countries in North Africa, Egypt, Libya and Ethiopia (Daniel 11:42-43). And he shall take from these countries gold, silver and precious ancient artifacts considered priceless to the world dating back to the days of the Pharaohs.

5. He will be at war with these North African nations, also the nations out of the far North and East will war against him (Daniel 11:44).

6. It could be that these nations will war against Mystery Babylon while the Anti-Christ is at war in North Africa.

7. His final military maneuver will be against Jerusalem. As he invades Jerusalem the remaining remnant of the Jews will scatter to the mountains and hills. At this time the greatest moment of Jewish history will unfold. Israel will repent and call upon Him whom they have rejected and crucified and confess Him as their Messiah (Zechariah 12:1-3; 14:1-2).

8. There are other possible military conquests by the Anti-Christ during Armageddon but I see them somewhat vague and insignificant.

HE IS THE CHRIST

This invasion of Jerusalem during Armageddon breaks the pride and rebellion of the Jewish people. The Jews repent of their sins and confess Jesus as their Messiah. The prophets described the remnant in repentance and mourning as the Anti-Christ and his army invade Jerusalem (Zechariah 12:10; Hosea 5:15).

In Matthew 23:39 Jesus laments over Jerusalem. In His earthly ministry Jerusalem repeatedly rejected the message of Jesus; therefore, He withdrew His presence and promised He would not be seen by them again until they would confess Him as their Messiah. *"...for I say to you, you shall see Me no more till you say, 'Blessed is He who comes in the name of the Lord!' "*.

When the Anti-Christ invades Jerusalem something finally causes the Jews to repent and confess Christ. Scripture does not reveal what caused their change of heart. Some speculate it could be the preaching of the 144,000 mentioned in Revelation, or perhaps the Two Witnesses, or the continued ministry of Elijah. However, it is not clearly stated. But, something finally penetrates the hardness of their heart and they confess Jesus!

> He withdrew His presence and promised He would not be seen by them again until they would confess Him as their Messiah.

As they confess Christ as their Messiah, Jesus then bursts through the clouds riding a white horse. It is astounding how fast Jesus answers their prayer once they call upon Him. John described what he saw in Revelation 19:11-16.

> [11]*"And I saw heaven opened, and behold a white horse; and he that sat upon him was called Faithful and True, and in righteousness he doth judge and make war.*
> [12] *His eyes were as a flame of fire, and on his head were*

> *many crowns; and he had a name written, that no man knew, but he himself.*
>
> *¹³ And he was clothed with a vesture dipped in blood: and his name is called The Word of God.*
>
> *¹⁴ And the armies which were in heaven followed him upon white horses, clothed in fine linen, white and clean.*
>
> *¹⁵ And out of his mouth goeth a sharp sword, that with it he should smite the nations: and he shall rule them with a rod of iron: and he treadeth the winepress of the fierceness and wrath of Almighty God.*
>
> *¹⁶ And he hath on his vesture and on his thigh a name written, KING OF KINGS AND LORD OF LORDS"* (KJV)

The Second Coming of Christ

This picture of Jesus bursting out of heaven on a white horse with the heavenly army following Him is the Second Coming of Christ. In Matthew chapter 6, Jesus taught His disciples to pray, *"Thy Kingdom come thy will be done IN earth as it is in heaven..."* (Matthew 6:10 KJV). This is the beginning of the answer to that prayer. The King has now come to the earth to set up His Kingdom, but first, He has to take care of some business! John the Revelator goes on to describe the scene in Revelation 19:17-20:3. I will summarize this great event:

The Anti-Christ (or the beast) and the kings of the earth with their armies gather to make war with Jesus and the army that is with Him. The army with Jesus represents all the Old Testament saints and the Church that was taken up in the rapture seven years prior. Among them are the millions of believers who have been martyred for the sake of Christ throughout all the ages. In this scene they are not the victims of "hate-filled blasphemers of

God"; they are the victors, riding white horses which is a symbol of power and strength!

Can you imagine the arrogance of the beast and the kings of the earth as they gather their army to war against Jesus? They are pictured as blundering fools. Their arrogance and deception is so deeply ingrained in their souls they actually think they can overcome Jesus the Son of God and the creator of the universe. It is the personification of stupidity, pride and defiance toward God Almighty.

The next scene is the moment we have all been waiting for. The Bible says, "*And the beast was taken, and with him the false prophet that wrought miracles*" (Revelation 19:20 KJV). They don't go 15 rounds, or 12, or even 3. There are no exchanges of fire or words, just one quick effortless swoosh...like a cat taking a mouse. Pounce, and they are both cast alive into a lake of fire burning with brimstone! And I will be right there to witness this great event and so will you if you have made Christ your Savior.

"...SHUT HIM UP"

It is not finished. Bear with me for a moment while I indulge myself in this incredible scene revealed by John! The next order of business is, "The Binding of Satan". John describes it thus, "*And I saw an angel come down from heaven having the key of the bottomless pit and a great chain in his hand. And he laid hold on the dragon, that old serpent, which is the devil, and Satan, and bound him 1,000 years. And cast him into the bottomless pit, and shut him up...*" I like the words, **"*...and shut him up.*"** It makes me feel good just to read these words. Say it out loud, it will make you feel better**..."Shut him up!"** I am looking to the day when the devil will finally have a muzzle put on his mouth in the same way a veterinarian would restrain a mad dog.

We have all suffered from the evil of this worldwide menace. The pain and suffering, the sickness and disease, the wars and rumors of wars that have devastated the world for six millennia has now come to a halt! The perpetrator of everything that is evil has met his fate and is now doomed to banishment and suffering for 1,000 years in the bottomless pit. "Hell", the Bible calls it, just where he belongs! Hallelujah! Hallelujah! What a glorious day it will be! Everyone will shout and breathe a sigh of relief!

JESUS THE VICTOR!

There is one more scene that needs to be addressed. It is revealed in Zechariah 14:3-4.

> ³"Then the Lord will go forth
> And fight against those nations,
> As He fights in the day of battle.
> ⁴ And in that day His feet will stand on the Mount of Olives,
> Which faces Jerusalem on the east.
> And the Mount of Olives shall be split in two,
> From east to west,
> Making a very large valley;
> Half of the mountain shall move toward the north
> And half of it toward the south."

Whenever great accomplishments are made in life there is some kind of victory stand that will be taken by the victor. In education there is graduation day when the student is recognized for his hard work and academic achievements. In the military there is the award ceremony when the soldier is presented medals of honor for his or her bravery and sacrifice. In sports it is press conferences, award banquets, and the Hall of Fame. In Nascar it is the victory lap followed by the trophy and roses, et cetera, et cetera.

When Jesus stands upon the Mount of Olives it is His victory ascent. Amazingly, it is the same piece of real estate where He sat 2,000 years before when He prophesied the destruction of Jerusalem to His disciples and gave the profound teaching about the signs of the times and the end of the age. It is not by chance that He returns to this spot for His victory ascent.

When He stands upon that mountain the mountain splits in two, half will move north and half will move south. Many have asked, "Why does He do this?" Simply because... He wants to! In this He will demonstrate to the world His omnipotence. He is all powerful. He has defeated His adversaries. He has come to rule the world with a rod of iron and nothing will stand in His way, not even the mountains. What a glorious day it will be!

The Millennial Reign of Christ

The destruction of the Anti-Christ, the false prophet and the binding of Satan will lead to the beginning of the Millennial Reign of Christ (Revelation 20:4). The Millennium refers to 1,000 years Christ will rule and reign on the earth. It was predicted by the Old Testament prophets such as Isaiah, Daniel, Micah and Zechariah.

Christ will rule and reign from the city of Jerusalem. Isaiah said the government will rest upon His shoulders (Isaiah 9:6). Those who have been faithful to the ministry of the Church, the resurrect-

> The perpetrator of everything that is evil has met his fate and is now doomed to banishment and suffering for 1,000 years in the bottomless pit.

ed Old Testament saints and those who were martyred for their faith during the Tribulation will rule with Him. The Bible says we will rule as Kings and Priests with Him (Revelation 5:10), as He rules with a rod of iron (Revelation 12:5).

Isaiah also spoke about a change in the animal kingdom, *"The wolf and the lamb shall feed together, and the lion shall eat straw like the bullock:..."* (Isaiah 65:25 KJV). Peace and safety will characterize this kingdom. Wild animals will be tame and harmony will exist.

It will not be a perfect world but it will be a far better existence than we could ever imagine. Because of the abiding presence of Christ the entire world will be dramatically changed. The study of the Millennial Reign of Christ is an amazing revelation in the Word of God. I have only touched on a few of the many great revelations of this soon coming Kingdom. I encourage you to further study of the scriptures about this subject. It will give you great hope for a world where Jesus is King, Satan is bound, and righteousness rules!

THE RELEASE OF SATAN

After Jesus rules for 1,000 years Satan will be loosed out of his prison. It is hard to imagine, but after everything that has already happened the great deceiver Satan, becomes a victim of his own devices. The deceiver is deceived into believing that he can yet defeat God. Not only is he deceived but he gathers a multitude of rebels the Bible once again identifies as Gog and Magog. They are many *"the number of whom is as the sand of the sea"* (Revelation 20:8 KJV).

I don't know about you but the very thought of this rebellion is enough to give me a mental hernia. How can it be possible for a people that have been ruled by the perfect Christ for 1,000 years decide to rebel against Him? The answer, at least in part, is found in biblical history. Lucifer's rebellion, the rejection and crucifixion of Christ in the first century, these blatant willful acts of rebellion against God Himself tell us that pride will cause some to reject even the perfection of the Almighty. This rebellion leads to the last and final war of all of the ages of man's existence according to Bible Prophecy.

THE FOURTH AND FINAL WAR

There is not much said about this last war (Revelation 20:7-9). In fact the whole war can be summed up with three thoughts:

1. The rebel forces are many; they are as numerous as the sand on the seashore. It is hard to imagine that there are that many stupid people on the planet. Perhaps this is why there has to be a hell! This rebellion reveals why Satan had to be released for a season, that he might draw out the rebellion and separate them before the establishment of the New Heaven and the New Earth.

2. They organize themselves around the beloved city which is the city of Jerusalem to make war.

3. Fire comes down from God out of heaven and devours them. And that is it! Glory to God! Nothing else is said!

> How can it be possible for a people that have been ruled by the perfect Christ for 1,000 years decide to rebel against Him?

There are many other great doctrines in the Bible that follow this last and final conflict. The Great White Throne Judgment. The New Heavens and the New Earth. I have plans to write on these subjects at a later time, but for now I want to close this chapter with some final thoughts.

"WHEN WILL THE END FINALLY COME?"

People often ask, "When will it happen? When will the end finally come?" Jesus answered this question in His Olivet Discourse when He was teaching on the signs of the times in Matthew 24:14. *"And this gospel of the kingdom shall be preached in all the world for a witness unto all nations; **and then shall the end come**"* (KJV author emphasis). Jesus said the End would come after the message of His return has been made known to the entire world. Not just any message, but specifically the message of His return which is the message of the Kingdom. Are you ready for that glorious day?

THE NEXT GREAT EVENT
THE RAPTURE

CHAPTER 4

I heard the Gospel preached for the first time in 1975. It was a life changing experience. What happened in my heart so many years ago was the beginning of the message in this book. In this chapter we'll take a look at what the Bible says about the return of Christ. But before we do I'd like to tell you about something that happened to me in the beginning of my journey with the Lord.

I was born and raised in the Catholic Church in the Greater New Orleans area in South Louisiana. Both my grandmothers were devout Catholics, as many southern people were during most of the 20th century. As a child I learned many great things about God in the Catholic Church. One of the most memorable experiences I had was during Lent. Every year for Lent, my grandmother took my sister and I to the "Way of the Cross", which began six weeks prior to Easter Sunday.

It was a special time, a very spiritual and moving experience in my childhood. Because of those experiences, I had a deep interest in the things of God from a very young age.

However, when I became a teen, I quickly turned into a rebel and became the "black sheep of the family." I left the church and my childhood experiences and turned to drugs, alcohol, rebellion and all the vices that go with that kind of destructive lifestyle.

In September of 1975, after two years of declining my Aunt Gail Cantrell's invitations to visit her church, I finally agreed to go. (Thank you Aunt Gail for taking me to church that Sunday!) I had never been in any other church besides a Catholic church. That morning she did her best to prepare me for what would be a turning point in my life.

In the Catholic Church there would be a reading of the Gospels during Mass, but there was never any preaching. I can honestly say that Sunday morning was the first time in my life, at age 19, that I had ever heard the preaching of the gospel. I was mesmerized by the preacher, Reverend Marvin Gorman. His words were powerful, spellbinding. It seemed as though every word he said was directed toward me, yet he knew nothing about me. At the end of the message he asked if anyone wanted to receive Jesus as their savior to raise their hand for prayer. Although I thought I had done this as a child, I felt a strong conviction on the inside to respond, so I did. That was the beginning of a transformation that would be the start of a lifetime commitment to the cause of Christ.

As I left church that morning, I was not exactly sure what had taken place but I knew in my heart I was different. From that Sunday to this day I have never gone back to that old lifestyle. God instantly and miraculously changed my life. In Bible terms, I became "Born Again." In a matter of days my entire life began to change. I rode a motorcycle at that time and the only Bible my family owned was one of those big family Bibles that, if you dropped it on your foot, you could hurt yourself. So I would strap that big Bible to the back of my motorcycle and off to church I'd go.

My friends and family thought I had jumped off the deep end, "The black sheep, what's he into now?". Some of my friends asked if I had done some bad drugs or something. Others would say, "he'll be back; give him a little time and it'll be Mark as usual." What they didn't understand, and neither did I at the time, was that what Jesus said to His disciples in John 15:16, *"You haven't chosen me but I have chosen you ..."*now applied to me. God had by His grace singled me out for a purpose. That purpose would soon be revealed to me in a most unusual way.

Jesus is Coming Back

About two months after my born again experience I was with a high school friend named Wayne. Wayne had been born again several years before me. I was shocked to find him in that Assembly of God church I had visited in my neighborhood where I grew up. Wayne was a God- send. He helped me adjust to my newfound life. He began spending time with me, sharing things he had learned about God and the Bible. I could listen to him for hours and I always had so many questions.

One day as Wayne and I were working under the hood of his car, he began to tell me about a film that was going to be at the church in a couple of weeks called "The Road to Armageddon." I asked him what the "Road to Armageddon" was. I had never heard such a term in my life. He began to tell me about this man named David Wilkerson who had done a documentary about a vision God had given him about all the things that would begin to happen in the U.S. leading up to the return of Christ.

I cannot explain what went on in my mind when he began to tell me that Jesus, the same Jesus I learned about in the Catholic Church as a child, was coming back! No one had ever told me Jesus was coming back to the earth. A few weeks later we watched this film by David Wilkerson and once again, like the first day I gave my heart to Christ, I was mesmerized by the message. It seemed as though I found the missing piece of the puzzle. Let me explain.

Life didn't make sense to me as a young man. I could not understand why so many people were so unhappy and had such mixed up lives, the young, the old, and everyone in between. It seemed everyone was discontent and filled with troubles and disappointment. I used to think, "God, either you made a mistake in creating all this mess or I missed something along the way." Well, God didn't make a mistake, but I sure did miss something.

That was over 37 years ago that I first heard the message about Christ' return. It greatly impacted my life then and it continues to be the single biggest motivator of my studies and my relentless pursuit of God for all these years. **Jesus is coming back!**

The Rapture of the Church

According to Biblical Prophecy the next prophetic word to be fulfilled is the rapture of the church. The word "rapture" is not found in the Bible. Amazingly, the word "Bible" is not in the Bible either. The word Rapture is derived from the Latin word *raptu* which means, "caught away or caught up." It is equivalent to the Greek word *harpaze*, translated as, **"caught up"** in I Thessalonians 4:17.

> *17 Then we who are alive and remain shall be **caught up** together with them in the clouds to meet the Lord in the air. And thus we shall always be with the Lord.* (emphasis author's)

Rapture is a term that describes one of the most exciting prophecies in God's Word. This prophecy explains what will happen to the Church (Christians) and to those who have already died in Christ (II Corinthians 5:17), or as Paul says are "asleep in Jesus." When this event takes place the dead in Christ will be raised in their glorified bodies. And believers still living at that time will be caught up together with them to meet the Lord in the air.

The Rapture is also referred to as the blessed hope. In Titus 2:13 the scripture says, *"Looking for the blessed hope and glorious appearing of our great God and Savior Jesus Christ"*. It is a blessed hope because of this great promise of the resurrection of the dead and the catching away of the people of God. This will happen before the Great Tribulation begins.

PICTURES AND TYPES

Many places in the Bible give us a picture of this great event. In Genesis chapter 6, we are told about a man called Noah. Noah lived in a time when the world had become so exceedingly wicked that God was going to destroy every living creature upon the face of the earth. But the Bible says, *"Noah found grace in the eyes of the Lord"* (Genesis 6:8), and because of Noah, a righteous man, God spared the earth from complete annihilation. The intervention of God in sparing Noah and his family is what Bible students call a "picture and type" of the Rapture.

God uses "pictures and types" throughout Scripture. They are similar to "analogies and metaphors," which means "one thing is likened to something else." The Biblical account of the story of Noah and his family being spared from the great flood is likened to the rapture of the church. God had Noah build an ark, which was a large boat, the first boat ever built. Noah put his family into the ark and God put every species of animal, male and female into the ark enabling them to survive the flood that came upon the entire world at that time in history. God brought judgment upon the ungodly but spared the righteous. Noah and his family experienced a type of the rapture. The entire world perished, but Noah and his family survived.

Another type of the rapture is also found in the book Genesis. It is the history of two cities, Sodom and Gomorrah. Once again the people of these cities had become so evil that God destroyed the cities with fire and brimstone. However, before He destroyed them, he sent angels into the city to take Lot and his family out before the destruction came by way of fire and brimstone. This too is a type of the rapture. Lot and his family survived but the ungodly were destroyed.

Jesus made reference to both of these historical events in Luke 17:26-28 *"And as it was in the days of Noah, so it will be also in the days of the Son of Man...Likewise as it was also in the days of Lot...Even so it will be in the day when the Son of Man is revealed".* You will also find this in Matthew 24:36-39 in the teaching of the signs of His return.

We find amazing similarities between the world of, *"the days of Noah and the days of Lot"* and our present world. This history also reveals how God will deliver the righteous from the judgment that is upon the horizon. The Theology for the Rapture is found in numerous places in the New Testament. My preferred reading is found in I Thessalonians 4:13-18. Here the Apostle Paul describes the events of the rapture in great detail.

> *¹³ But I do not want you to be ignorant, brethren, concerning those who have fallen asleep, lest you sorrow as others who have no hope.*
> *¹⁴ For if we believe that Jesus died and rose again, even*

so God will bring with Him those who sleep in Jesus.
15 For this we say to you by the word of the Lord, that
we who are alive and remain until the coming of the
Lord will by no means precede those who are asleep.
16 For the Lord Himself will descend from heaven with
a shout, with the voice of an archangel, and with the
trumpet of God. And the dead in Christ will rise first.
17 Then we who are alive and remain shall be caught
up together with them in the clouds to meet the Lord
in the air. And thus we shall always be with the Lord.
18 Therefore comfort one another with these words.

1 Thessalonians 4:13-18

FIVE SIGNIFICANT POINTS FROM THESE SCRIPTURES:

1. "The Lord Himself shall descend from heaven"
2. "...With a shout, with the voice of the archangel and with the trumpet of God"

3. "...The dead in Christ will rise first"

4. "...We who are alive and remain shall be caught up together with them in the clouds to meet the Lord in the air"

5. "...And so shall we ever be with the Lord"

In a few short words written by the Apostle many years ago, these scriptures reveal a wealth of wisdom and insight about the eternal future of the Believer. I will briefly expound on the significant points.

1. ***"The Lord Himself shall descend from heaven."*** Jesus is coming back! He will not allow things on earth to continue as they are. Just the other day I saw a headline

on a news program that read, "The World is Broke." This is true. The world is broke beyond man's ability to fix what is wrong. I get somewhat amused as I listen to the arrogance of man as he continually tries to fix what has been broken without the intervention of God.

Within the heart of man he longs for things to be right. Something inside of us objects to the terrible things happening around us day by day. We also know, inside our heart, that the world cannot continue as it is. We know and feel these things because God created us this way.

In this descent of Jesus from heaven (The Rapture), He will not put His foot on the earth, He will appear in the clouds only to those who know Him and are prepared for His return. In the **"Second coming of Christ",** He will be riding a white horse and the saints of God who were caught up into heaven in the rapture will be coming back with Him (Revelation 19:11-16). There is a space of at least seven years between these two events. **It is important that the reader does not confuse the Rapture with the Second Coming of Christ.**

The Rapture will be the single most exciting event since the virgin birth of Jesus, His ministry and resurrection two thousand years ago! The Rapture is imminent! The term *"imminence"* as applied to the Rapture of the Church, means that Christ may return at any moment for His church. There is no biblical prophecy or event that must happen before the Rapture takes place. All has been fulfilled that needs to be fulfilled prior to the Rapture. Notice the words *"The Lord Himself shall descend."* He will not send angels for this great intervention in the history of man; Jesus Himself will come to receive His church. It can happen at any moment! Are you ready for His return?

2. ***"With a shout, with the voice of the archangel and with the trumpet of God".*** In the book of Joshua, chapter six, God gave Joshua instructions as to how Israel would bring down the walls of Jericho after they crossed the Jordan River and entered the Promised Land. This is an amazing history about how God's covenant people would cross a great river by the intervention of God. And after the crossing, they would conquer and possess the land by a miraculous intervention of God.

The word of the Lord to Joshua in 6:5 (KJV) is another Old Testament picture and type of the events that take place during the rapture; "*And it shall come to pass, that when they make a long blast with the ram's horn, and when ye hear the sound of the trumpet, all the people shall shout with a great shout; and the wall of the city shall fall down flat, and the people shall ascend up every man straight before him*". **Notice the words "trumpet…shout…the people shall ascend up."**

The Apostle Paul said concerning the Old Testament (I Corinthians 10:11), "*Now all these things happened to them as examples, and they were written for our admonition, upon whom the ends of the ages have come*". Can you imagine how Joshua must have felt when God said to him that the walls of Jericho would come down with a shout and the blowing of the trumpet? According to Paul, some of these strange ways of doing things in the Old Testament were done for our admonition. Reason being, it helps the reader to authenticate the New Testament message as truly being from God because it resembles what God has done in past history with His covenant people.

In Joshua's conquest it was the people who shouted and blew the trumpet. In the rapture, it will be the heavenly host. Do you know that in heaven two angels have been given an assignment?

One will give a shout that will be heard throughout the whole earth, by the living and the dead, and the other will blow a trumpet. Knowing how close the rapture is, I would say those angels must be taking breathing lessons anxiously awaiting their command from the Father to let it loose! Will all hear?

> Jesus Himself will come to receive His church. It can happen at any moment! Are you ready for His return?

No! Only those who are prepared and ready for His return will hear the shout and the sound of the trumpet. Will you hear, are you ready for His return?

3. *"The dead in Christ will rise first."* Now the "Blessed Hope" begins to come into focus. Paul said, *"But I do not want you to be ignorant, brethren, concerning those who have fallen asleep, lest you sorrow as others who have no hope."* To be ignorant is to be unlearned. We put learning at a high premium in our present world system. I am amazed that, in the age where knowledge and learning are at the forefront in one's pursuit for success, so many can be so uneducated about their eternal destiny. Even in the church world I find precious few who have a working knowledge of the doctrines that concern our eternal abode.

Paul had many titles, Apostle, Servant, and he even referred to himself as a Prisoner of Jesus Christ, which emphasized his total submission to God's plan for his life. He was also a gifted teacher, who by way of revelation from God revealed the doctrine for the New Testament Church. Within that revelation of the church we have the teachings of Christ's return. It was obvious that understanding was of utmost importance to Paul when he said, "I do not want you to be ignorant."

Paul made it clear to the church what awaits those who have been laid to rest. He doesn't say they have "Passed away" or "Died," but he referred to them as being *"Asleep."* What a comforting way to think of those who have gone on before us. The Apostle clarified this profound truth in his letter to the Corinthians, *"We are confident, yes, well pleased rather to be absent from the body and to be present with the Lord"* (II Corinthians 5:8).

When a Believer breathes his last breath in this life, his body is laid in a grave. His spirit and soul go on to be with the Lord, in heaven, awaiting the resurrection of the body. Although the body goes back into the ground from which it came, that dead body will be resurrected when the Rapture takes place. Man is a triune being (body, soul and spirit) and the redemption of man includes body, soul and spirit.

In I Corinthians 15:35, Paul answers a question that many have today. *" But someone will say, "How are the dead raised up? And with what body do they come?"* What a question! How are the dead raised and what kind of body will they have? Have you ever considered what your body will look like throughout eternity? Throughout the remainder of this chapter in I Corinthians the Apostle goes on to teach one of the most profound truths about eternal life you will ever find in scripture as it pertains to the body. I could write volumes on this one chapter but that is not my intent in this study. I will, however, give you some food for thought.

Have you ever considered why Jesus was crucified and died at approximately 33 and a half years of age? Modern science helps answer this theological mystery. Science tells us that the human body reaches physical maturity at about 33 years old, approximately the age Jesus was crucified and died. After we reach our early 30's the body slowly enters into a dying process. This is not encouraging but it is true. Professional athletes prove this science to be true. If you know anything about sports, an athlete will reach his peak performance in his early 30's, with the exception of injuries.

You're probably wondering what does this have to do with our subject. Everything, I believe we will live out eternity in our body similar to as we were when we were in our early 30's, with the exception of sickness, disease, handicaps or any other abnormality that would have been the result of the fall of man. In I Corinthians 15:42-44 Paul says, *"...The body is sown in corruption* (or death*), it is raised in incorruption* (or eternal*). It is sown in dishonor, it is raised in glory. It is sown in weakness, it is raised in power. It is sown a natural body, it is raised a spiritual body."*

This is truly the **"Blessed Hope."** It is a great challenge to live in a body that is in a dying process. We pray for the sick. We believe according to scripture that God has provided healing for our sick bodies. In James 5:14-16 we are commanded to pray for the sick. I have seen God heal hundreds of people in over 30 years of ministry. In fact if it weren't for the ministry of healing and miracles, some of us would have already gone on to be with the Lord. But God intervened with His miraculous power; you still have life and are reading this book because of His intervention. However, there is one sickness which God will not heal and that is death and dying. Eventually, everyone will die. Death is an appointment according to scripture (Hebrews 9:27). Or shall we say as Paul, we will all fall asleep one day.

> [27] *"And as it is appointed for men to die once, but after this the judgment"*

In the Rapture of the church, *"the dead in Christ will rise first."* All who have died in faith with Jesus as their savior will come out of the grave with an incorruptible body which they will have for all eternity. Another thought I find to be amazing about the resurrection of the dead is revealed in I Corinthians 15:52. And that is the speed in which this will take place. It will all happen *"In a moment, in the twinkling of an eye..."* Now that's fast. How quickly these dying weak bodies will be changed into the glorious body He has prepared for us. Are you ready for your immortal, incorruptible, glorious resurrected body?

To give better insight as to what kind of body it will be, we must look at Jesus after His resurrection. He could be seen; He could eat; He could walk through closed doors, and yet He said to Thomas, *"Reach your finger here, and look at My hands; and reach your hand here, and put it into My side..."* (John 20:27). He could be felt by another. He could translate himself from one place to the next with only a thought (Luke 24:13-35) Wow! Sounds like a modern day superhero created in the world of fantasy. This is no fantasy. This is the "Blessed Hope" of our eternal existence with the God who gave His Son to die for us.

Perhaps this great revelation gives meaning to Romans 8:18 (KJV) when Paul said, *"For I reckon that the sufferings of this present time are not worthy to be compared with the glory that shall be revealed in us"*. Many of you reading this book are suffering with sickness and disease, and some are even dying. You have lost your health, and life has become like a hell on earth, a mere existence that has caused you to question if God really cares and loves you. Many have been

> Hold on to your fraith, and lift your head high for His return is closer than you think.

prayed for more times than you can count but you continue to suffer with sickness in your body. Questions race through your mind leaving you in confusion, disillusionment and fear. Night times are especially difficult, and you wrestle with anger deep within your soul as you try to hold on to your faith and not become overwhelmed with anger and bitterness.

My dear friend, please be encouraged by this hope and promise. The things you are suffering are not worthy to be compared with the glorious body that awaits you in the resurrection. Look to the future. Hold on to this precious promise. In just a short time your suffering will cease and you will receive the most wonderful life of health, joy, and most of all you will see Him who loves you face to face. Now that is worth waiting for! So for now, hold on to your faith, and lift your head high for His return is closer than you think.

4. ***"We who are alive and remain shall be caught up together with them in the clouds to meet the Lord in the air."*** The words, *"we who are alive and remain"* speak of the church, the believer. The promise is that *"we shall be caught up together with them in the clouds to meet the Lord in the air."*

Let us review the sequence of events Paul has revealed to this point in our study:

- The Lord descends from heaven
- One angel shouts
- Another angel sounds the trumpet
- The dead are raised
- The believer is caught up (raptured) as the dead are raised

As the dead burst out of their graves, in a moment's time, the Believer who is subject to mortality (meaning death and dying) will be changed. In I Corinthians 15:53 Paul said, *"Corruptible must put on incorruption, and this mortal must put on immortality."*

Can you picture in your mind this supernatural event? The graveyards that house millions of bodies of believers who have already passed from this life will have to give up those dead bodies to be resurrected just as Jesus was resurrected 2,000 years ago. Then the dedicated believer who is walking with God will be caught up with them to meet the Lord in the air!

Let's use our imagination for a few moments. With the help of the Spirit of God consider the impact this will have on the entire world. For the dead in Christ and the Believer this will be a glorious moment, but for the rest of the world it will be a crisis unparalleled to anything ever known to man since the beginning of time.

Let us consider just a few of the ways the world will be impacted by this event:

- Cemeteries will look like bombs have been dropped on them. Mausoleums, graves, tombs will be broken into pieces.
- Believers from all over the world will vanish in the blink of an eye.
- Jesus said in Matthew 24:41, *"Two women will be grinding at the mill: one will be taken and the other left."*.
- Babies and children will vanish right before the eyes of childcare workers.
- Highways, interstates and streets in your subdivision will have vehicles crashing for the lack of drivers. These accidents will cause a chain reaction of explosions and the spill of toxic waste.

- Planes will crash as pilots vanish from the cockpit.

- Airports will be in pandemonium as not only pilots disappear but also traffic controllers from their control towers.

- Trains will crash carrying every kind of cargo imaginable including passenger trains filled with people.

- Nuclear power plants managed by people will become volatile in just a few hours time.

- The impact will dismantle governments and their military and will cause economic collapse worldwide.

The list is endless. In just moments the entire world will be a disaster and chaotic mess. In the U.S. alone if only 10% (approximately 30 million people) of the population go up in the Rapture, America as we know it, will cease to exist. The government will collapse; the military will collapse; and whatever is left of the economy at that time will also collapse.

How will the world respond to such a disaster? What will the media and political leaders around the world have to say? I'm going to suggest a few of the obvious reactions.

LEFT BEHIND

In the religious world there will be many who have heard countless preachers like me warn the world about this event. Yet they gave no credibility to these warnings. In spite of what they heard, they continued to live as though God doesn't exist. They will remember the message, and in a moments time will realize what has taken place. They will also realize they have been left behind. Remember the day of Noah. The warning came but they would not heed. Millions died in the flood of Noah's day!

Backslidden preachers, seminary professors, Sunday school teachers, and others who are in church every Sunday but are not living with a genuine faith in God will fall to the ground and weep uncontrollably when they realize they have been left behind. You may ask why would you say that about people who are doing religious work? Because of what the Bible says, *"For by grace you are saved through faith; and that not of yourselves: it is a gift of God. Not of works least any man should boast"* (Ephesians 2:8-9). Religious works will not save anyone!

WHAT ABOUT THE CHILDREN?

Often I am asked this question, "Will the children go up in the Rapture?" Children are born innocent; they have neither accepted Christ as their savior, nor rejected Him. There comes a time in the life of every child when they will have to make a decision about Christ. We call it the "Age of Accountability." It is the age when a child knows the difference between right and wrong and chooses Christ. The thought is consistent with sound Biblical doctrine. Only God knows when a particular child will reach the age of accountability.

I am not concerned about the innocent. I am concerned about the generation of this present time which is not following in the faith of their fathers. In the beginning of this chapter we mentioned how the days leading up to the return of Christ would be as it was in the "Days of Noah." Have you ever considered why only eight people were spared in Noah's day?

From the time God first commanded Noah to build the ark to the appointed time of the flood was 120 years. The Bible says only Noah, his wife, his three sons and their wives survived the flood safely inside the ark, eight people. Peter made reference to this when he said "...*few, that is, eight souls were saved*" speaking of the days of Noah (I Peter 3:20). My question is, what happened to Noah's grandchildren, or his great grandchildren, or great, great grandchildren? In 120 years there could have been six or more generations born to Noah and his sons. And Noah was 600 years old when the flood took place. Where are the descendents of Noah? Why were there only eight in the ark?

Jesus said it would once again be like it was in the days of Noah. Noah failed to pass his faith on beyond one generation. His sons, and today's world is no different. We are not passing on our faith to our children and grandchildren. This is a sobering thought! This is what Jesus said the world would be like before His return.

Many will be left behind including some we love the most. Some of you are reading this book because a loving friend or relative put it in your hands. The question you must wrestle with is, **"Is the message you are reading at this very moment an opportunity given to you by God to prepare you for this great event?"** A friend or relative may have put the book in your hand but the message

> In 120 years there could have been six or more generations born to Noah and his sons. And Noah was 600 years old when the flood took place. Where are the descendents of Noah? Why were there only eight in the ark?

didn't come from them. Neither did it come from the author. The message has come by way of God, the Holy Spirit to you at this very moment of your life to prepare you for that which is about to unfold in this present time of world history.

It would be a good time for you to pause and ask the Lord as the Apostle Paul did many years ago when Jesus spoke to him on the Road to Damascus *"Lord, what will you have me to do"*? Please understand, only your personal faith in Christ can prepare you for this day. The faith of your parents or grandparents cannot save you. It is a personal decision you have to make for yourself!

THE WORLD WILL BE DESPERATE FOR ANSWERS!

After the Rapture takes place, world leaders will look to scientists for answers. For decades we have had testimonies from credible people, some in our military and law enforcement, who have testified of UFO sightings, which I believe are manifestations of demons. A quick scientific and political answer will be the possibility of abductions from some alien invasion.

Modern day science continues to lead the world into believing that there is life somewhere else in the universe. This will give credibility to their theories. One of the educational channels recently had a two hour special about what would happen to our world if suddenly there were no people. How incredible! We are in the last moments of history leading up to the Rapture of the church and science is theorizing about what would happen to the earth if all the people suddenly vanished. Just a coincidence....?

THE STAGE IS BEING SET

All these theories being presented by modern day scientists represent a strategy of the devil to use this event to set the stage for the next deception on the horizon which is a "One World Government" and the rise of the Antichrist.

Some of you reading this book will humble yourself, hear the message and join the millions who will be caught up in the Rapture. Others reading right now will hear and not necessarily disagree but will have a passive attitude and put off what needs to be done now. You will not feel the urgency to repent and make peace with God now! And by putting it off you will miss the Rapture. Others will laugh and mock, harden your heart saying we are doomsday prophets and religious fanatics and ignore the message, and in doing so will suffer the devastating consequences of being left behind.

Dear reader, don't wait another moment to make peace with God! Jesus could come back before you read the next chapter. Listen to your heart not just your head. The Spirit of Christ wants to speak to you at this very moment, if you will turn the ear of your heart to Him. In Revelation chapter 3 verse 20 Jesus spoke to the church at Laodicea and said, " *Behold, I stand at the door and knock. If anyone hears My voice and opens the door, I will come in to him and dine with him, and he with Me.*"

> Do you hear His soft gentle knock? He will not bust the door down; He knocks. Only you can open the door and let Him in.

The door is the door of your heart. Jesus has been knocking for a long time. Do you hear His soft gentle knock? He will not bust the door down; He knocks. Only you can open the door and let Him in. Before you go any further, if you have not already done it, put the book down and in your own words ask Him to forgive you of your sins and come into your heart and be your Lord and Savior. You will not be disappointed. He will hear your prayer, forgive your sins and write your name in the Lamb's book of life, which leads to the next great truth in this amazing study of God's word.

5. ***"And so shall we ever be with the Lord"*** Can you imagine leaving this earth, leaving behind sickness, pain, suffering, death, dying, wars, conflict and on and on. This is a *"Blessed Hope."* The Apostle Paul had such a vivid revelation of the life hereafter that in his writing to the church at Philippi he wrote *"For me to live is Christ and to die is gain"* (Philippians 1:21).

When Paul said *"to live is Christ"*, he was speaking of his identity with Christ in his ministry to the church. Then he said *"to die is gain."* Paul knew that the life that was yet to come was a greater life not a lesser life. In verses 23 and 24 of Philippians Chapter one, he spoke of the struggle in his soul to depart from this life to forever be with Christ. But the overwhelming responsibility he carried in his soul was to remain here on earth and continue his ministry to the church. Thank God he continued to persevere and minister to the church.

What will life be like when we leave this earth in the Rapture to forever be with the Lord? We find the answer in the book of Revelation. The Apostle John wrote the book of Revelation on the Isle of Patmos in approximately 90 – 96 A.D. Revelation is the last book in the New Testament and the most unusual book in the entire Bible. It is call the "Apocalypse" which is a word derived from the Greek word *apocalupsis,* which is translated "revelation" in respect to its message which is the "Revelation of Jesus Christ" or the revealing of Jesus Christ to the world.

The world has never seen Jesus in all His glory. In His ministry on earth Jesus set aside His glory and took upon Himself the form of a servant, and was made in the likeness of men (Philippians 2:7). He was 100% man, 100% God. He was *Emmanuel*, God with us! But He came as a servant to die for the sins of the whole world.

In Revelation He is revealed to the world as the King of Kings and the Lord of Lords (Revelation 19:16). In Revelation 4:1 John the revelator said, *"After these things I looked, and behold, a door standing open in heaven. And the first voice which I heard like a trumpet speaking with me, saying, Come up here, and I will show you things which must take place after this."*

This is the "Rapture of the Church." When Jesus said to John,

"...*come up here*", John was taken up into heaven. This represents the Church being taken up out of the world before the seven years of the Great Tribulation begins. All the background I have given you is for this purpose. What John saw, as he was taken up into heaven, is what every believer will see when the Rapture takes place as is revealed in Revelation chapters 4 and 5. You must read it for yourself. It is a breathtaking revelation of what John saw and what every believer will see when we leave this world to forever be with the Lord.

THREE STEPS TO ETERNAL DESTINY

I see three progressions for the Believer as revealed in the Bible:

1. **The first life, our natural birth,** the life we have now, we are the sons of Adam, subject to death and dying because of Adam's sin that has been passed on to all men (Romans 5:12).

2. **Our second life or second birth,** through repentance and the Born Again experience we reign with Christ for 1,000 years (The Millennium) after the Rapture and the seven year Great Tribulation period. This is called the Millennial Reign. The Millennial Reign is a better life because Jesus will reign as King and we will reign with Him in our immortal bodies, no longer subject to death and dying.

3. **Our eternal destiny,** the final revelation according to scripture, is found in Revelation 21:1- 6. It is the new heaven and the new earth for the first heaven and earth will pass away. At this time God Himself will be with His people and John said, *"God shall wipe away all tears*

from their eyes; and there shall be no more death, nei-
ther sorrow, nor crying, neither shall there be any more
pain: for the former things are passed away."

This is our final destiny according to scripture. No more death, dying, sickness, disease, suffering and pain. Time will cease to exist. He will be our God and we shall be His people in complete harmony with Him.

SUMMARY

God has a plan, an eternal plan for man and that means you! The rapture of the church is imminent. Jesus is soon to return for His church, *" For God hath not appointed us to wrath, but to obtain salvation by our Lord Jesus Christ,"* (I Thessalonians 5:9 KJV). For the born again believer it will be an exciting existence as we shall forever be with our Lord. For the non-believer there will be an eternal existence separated from God in a devil's hell. My hope and prayer is to reach out to as many people as possible in this life that they too may take part in the rapture and spend eternity with Jesus.

Many years ago I was sharing Christ with a young man that was lost. He did not know Christ or what it meant to be born again. I asked him where he planned on spending eternity, heaven or hell. He said to me with a laugh, "Man we are already in hell, this miserable place is hell." I said to him you are right, for the believer that is. For the born again believer this life is the nearest we will ever get to a devil's hell. However, for the person who has not received Christ as his savior, this is your heaven!

Angrily, he retorted back to me, "What do you mean? Are you saying this life is my heaven and your hell?" I said, "Yes, for the believer this is my hell. For the non-believer this is the closest thing to heaven you will ever experience." He didn't like that analogy because life had been hard on him and he had not experienced the forgiveness of sins and knowing God as his heavenly Father.

I wish I could say that young man received Christ that day; he did not, at least not in my presence. But thank God for His eternal word that will never return to Him void. As I prayed for that young man to find Christ some time in his life, so I pray for everyone who is reading this book. If you have not met our Lord and Savior Jesus Christ, the Son of God, call on Him. He will make Himself known to you and forever change your life.

SIGNS OF THE TIMES

CHAPTER 5

In this chapter we will enter into one of the most enlightening parts of this study, the "Signs of the Times." The Bible gives us many "signs" that represent the way by which God would direct us throughout history that we may know where we are at a given time on God's prophetic time table.

In the Bible, the word "sign" and its literal meaning is used as a metaphor to communicate truth. During Jesus' earthly ministry He used things we are familiar with to teach us great mysteries about His soon coming Kingdom. One of the most common ways He did this was to teach with parables. You will notice in the Gospels that Jesus often began teaching with the words, *"The kingdom of heaven is like unto…"*. He would then give a parable, which is an illustrated story to teach the truth He wanted to communicate.

Signs are a part of our everyday life. Consider for a moment, when you are driving on the Interstate Highways, you will look for the signs to get where you are going. North, South, East and West, they all speak regarding which direction you are traveling. The sign also tells you where you are, or how close or how far away you are from your destination. The "signs of the times" do the same for us concerning the things that pertain to our eternal destiny and that which is coming upon the world in the last days. Jesus said there would be signs in the End Times that would tell us just how close we would be to His return.

We will begin in Matthew 16:1-4.

> *[1]"Then the Pharisees and Sadducees came, and testing Him asked that He would show them a sign from heaven. [2] He answered and said to them, "When it is evening you say, 'It will be fair weather, for the sky is red'; [3] and in the morning, 'It will be foul weather today, for the sky is red and threatening.' Hypocrites! You know how to discern the face of the sky, but you cannot discern the signs of the times. [4] A wicked and adulterous generation seeks after a sign, and no sign shall be given to it except the sign of the prophet Jonah." And He left them and departed.*

A brief summary of the background of this chapter in Matthew's account of the life of Jesus will be helpful. At this time in Biblical history Jesus' fame was now spreading throughout the countryside of Judea. He had performed many miracles. He healed the sick; the blind could see; the lame could walk; the deaf could hear; the dead were raised back to life and demons were cast out. On two separate occasions he fed thousands by miraculously multiplying a few fish and an armful of bread. He had become very popular with the average everyday people because of His miracles and teaching about His Father's kingdom. But He quickly became the enemy of the religious leaders of the day.

The Pharisees and Sadducees were the two most prominent religious groups of the day. Although they had opposing views about Old Testament law, when it came to this new religion with a leader by the name of Jesus, they joined forces in opposition against Him. The Scripture says in Matthew 16 that shortly after Jesus miraculously fed the multitudes, *"Then the Pharisees and Sadducees came, and testing Him, they asked that He would show them a sign from heaven."*

What audacity they had to ask Him to show them a sign! He had already shown them so many miraculous signs they could not be numbered. But I see something in this text that is very significant to the world in which we live. Please follow me closely in what I am about to say.

SHOW US A SIGN

The religious leaders were asking Jesus to show them a sign. Jesus' response was unexpected; he rebuked them for their request. Jesus said to them, *"When it is evening you say, it will be fair weather, for the sky is red; and in the morning, it will be foul weather today, for the sky is red and threatening."* The first time I read this scripture many years ago, it got my attention. As a young man I was a fisherman on the Gulf coast of Louisiana. I am a Merchant Marine Officer and Licensed Boat Captain with the U.S. Coast Guard. I learned this proverbial saying to be true just as other mariners across the world, by experience! As fishermen we learned to live by this weather phenomenon. Although we have changed the wording some, it has the same meaning. Today we say it this way, "Red in the morning is a sailor's warning, red at night is a sailor's delight." All mariners know this from experience.

Look at Jesus' next statement. What an attention getter! *"Hypocrites! You know how to discern the face of the sky, but you cannot discern the signs of the times."* Jesus was not happy! He was angered by the religious leaders who did not know what time it was on God's prophetic timetable.

113

Jesus Was the Sign

The ones Jesus referred to as hypocrites were asking for a sign. **Had they known the prophetic scriptures concerning the coming of the Messiah, they would not have been asking to see a sign; they would have been bowing down to the sign, because Jesus was the sign!** They were looking at the sign; the sign was talking to them and they were still asking for a sign. Had they been more attentive to the prophecies about the coming Messiah, they would have known He was the promised one. Jesus the Messiah, the son of the living God was the greatest sign since the creation of the world.

In Luke's gospel chapter 2:34, Simeon addressed Mary and Joseph in the temple and called Jesus "a sign!" Simeon recognized Him as a sign but the religious leaders refused to recognize Him, or perhaps they knew it, but had too much religious pride to admit that He was the one.

Now let's take a closer look at the teaching of Jesus in Matthew chapter 24. It is called by Biblical scholars "The Olivet Discourse", a term we will use throughout our study. In this discourse with Jesus and His disciples, many important things concerning the signs of the time are revealed.

Many details about the signs of Christ' return are found in both Old and New Testament writings. If you were to exhaust every reference about the signs of the times, an element of mystery still remains. This is common with the study of all biblical truth. That is why Bible study requires a humble heart that remains fixed on the Lord Himself. Remember this as you continue. Your study should cause you to love Him and fear Him with a humble heart. If this is not achieved, then we have truly missed the objective of this great study of God's word!

WHAT WILL BE THE SIGN OF YOUR COMING, AND THE END OF THE WORLD?

"The end of the world!" "Armageddon!" "The Apocalypse!" "The End of Days!" "Doomsday!" The movie industry has capitalized on this theme for more than half a century. It makes for good science fiction. But in the context of Bible Prophecy it is not sci-fi, it is the single most important subject of study in our day.

The question: *"What will be the sign of your coming?"* Jesus gave 11 signs in Matthew 24:2-14, which represent the signs at the end of the age. When I read these signs, I see Jesus the Savior of the world, and in this case the prophet of God, standing on the shoreline of eternity waiving a flag trying to get our attention signifying the nearness of the Rapture and the things that will follow. Do you see the distress flags waiving in the hands of our savior? They can be called the general signs of the course of this age leading up to His return. I will list these 11 signs for quick reference. Then we will give a brief overview of each of them in the light of current events in our modern world.

1. The destruction of the temple
2. Deception
3. Wars and rumors of wars
4. Famines
5. Pestilence
6. Earthquakes
7. Persecution
8. Offense
9. False Prophets
10. The Absence of Love
11. A Promise and the Mandate of the church

He was angered by the religious leaders who did not know what time it was on God's prophetic timetable.

Please note: It does not take a historian to know that these things (signs) we are about to study have been taking place for the past 2,000 years and beyond. In I Thessalonians chapter 5 Paul gives us insight about the signs that will be evident in the "Day of the Lord."

"The Day of the Lord" represents a period of time after the Rapture of the Church, which includes the Great Tribulation period. **I believe we are standing in the doorway of "The Day of the Lord", and because of this, the signs of the times are already beginning to come into focus.**

Paul said in I Thessalonians 5:3, *"For when they say, 'Peace and safety!' then sudden destruction comes upon them, as labor pains upon a pregnant woman. And they shall not escape."* Paul compares the signs of the times in the Day of the Lord to be like a woman in labor pains. There are three things about a woman having labor pains that are significant to recognizing the sign of the times.

1. When a woman goes into labor, the initial pains are gentle and then progress to greater and more intense levels of pain.

2. As the pains get greater, they also get closer together.

3. As in normal child birth, once the labor pains begin there is no turning back. In a short time a child will be born. Paul said this is what will happen in the end time. The signs will become greater in magnitude and they will be closer together through the passing of time. Also, notice the words, *"And they shall not escape."* Just as the mother will not escape giving

birth, we will not escape that which the Bible says will come forth.

WE ARE NOT APPOINTED TO WRATH

The Church will escape the wrath of God which is the Great Tribulation period mentioned in Matthew 24:21, by way of the Rapture. In I Thessalonians 5:9 (KJV) Paul said, " *For God hath not appointed us to wrath,*". Wrath is not the appointment of the believer.

However, Paul strongly emphasized that we will not escape many of the cataclysmic events that will take place as the "Signs of the times" begin to climax. At this present time we are beginning to experience the *"sudden destruction"* Paul wrote about in I Thessalonians 5:3. How intense these things will become before the Rapture is not clearly revealed in scripture. **The teaching of the Rapture of the church does not lead us to believe we will escape all tribulation and difficulty as the end draws near. But we will escape the "Great Tribulation" revealed in the book of Revelation.**

I. THE DESTRUCTION OF THE TEMPLE

> [2] *"...Assuredly, I say to you, not one stone shall be left here upon another, that shall not be thrown down."*
> Matthew 24:2

The first prophetic sign Jesus gave was the destruction of the temple in the city of Jerusalem. *"...Assuredly, I say to you, not one stone shall be left here upon another, that shall not be thrown down"*. This was the first sign of the Olivet discourse. History reveals that in 70 A.D. the Romans invaded the city of Jerusalem and destroyed the temple and, just as Jesus said, "not one stone was left upon another." The entire city was destroyed by the Romans.

Jesus' prophecy was literally fulfilled. When the Romans burned the temple the extreme heat of the fire caused the gold inside of the temple to melt. As the gold melted it dripped between the mortar and the stones that made up the structure of the temple. Later the soldiers went back and literally broke apart every stone of the temple to extract the gold that had lodged between the cracks in the stones, thus fulfilling Jesus' prophecy, "not one stone was left upon another." The other signs that Jesus mentioned in Matthew 24 would never be seen by Jesus' disciples and the first century church. These are the signs that are beginning to manifest in our present world, which is the end of the age, the day in which we live.

The destruction of the temple by the Romans in 70 A.D. marked a very significant time in Prophetic history. I will make reference to it many times throughout the writing of this book. For the student of Eschatology it is a very important event to remember as you will see in the following chapters.

II. DECEPTION AND FALSE PROPHETS

> 4 "...Take heed that no one deceives you. 5 For many will come in My name, saying, 'I am the Christ,' and WILL deceive many...11 Then many false prophets will rise up and deceive many."
>
> Matthew 24:4-5, 11

I will address deception and false prophets together (#2 and #9 in the list previously mentioned in this chapter). In verses 4 and 5 Jesus said, "Take heed that no one deceives you. For many will come in my name saying I am the Christ, and will deceive many." Jesus is talking about a worldwide religious deception, and in verse 11 He said, "And many false prophets shall arise and deceive many."

Throughout the world there are many false religions. I found one report that said there are over 750 million identifiable religions worldwide. That is not hard to believe because in Genesis chapter four there are only four people on the earth and two different religious beliefs. The first two men that we have record of practicing religion are Cain and Abel; the difference in their belief caused one to murder the other. How amazing, four people, two religions, the first murder and the first religious war!!!

Deception in the simplest definition is when you believe a lie as though it were the truth. Deception must have a vehicle, and the vehicle is the false prophet. There are many false prophets in the world today spreading their deception at an alarming rate. Modern technology makes this easier than ever before. We have always had false prophets. Paul had to deal with them during his ministry and every Biblical leader since his time has had his fair share of false prophets and their deception to contend with.

FALSE PROPHETS IN THE CHURCH

The writers of the New Testament warned about the rise of false prophets and false teachers within the church. Jude said in verse 4 (KJV), *"For there are certain men crept in unawares."* When I read those words I think of a snake slithering in below the radar unnoticed until it is right in the middle of your house.

> Deception in the simplest definition is when you believe a lie as though it were the truth.

Paul prophesied to the believers in Thessalonica, that before there would be the revealing of the Anti-Christ, there would first be a *"…Falling away"* within the church (II Thessalonians 2:3). The Falling Away is the End Time Apostasy of the church, and this too is a sign of the times. This is happening right now in the U.S. The statistics of church closings and the decline in church attendance are staggering. They serve as proof that this prophecy is being fulfilled daily. And you will notice a direct correlation between the End Time Apostasy and the rise of the False Teachers and False Prophets.

Recently, I was watching such a person on one of the religious cable networks. I had known from the first time I watched this man that he was a false prophet, but I wanted to listen to what he was peddling on this particular broadcast. I have always been amazed by how many gullible people follow these false teachers.

As I was watching and listening, I was surprised at the level of influence he had in his presentation. He was making an appeal for a $1,000 gift from all those who wanted to become the next millionaires. You will notice as you listen to the False Prophet, they obsessively use the words "The Lord told me". It is remarkable that every time the Lord "speaks" to them it involves some means of net gain to their personal ministry.

As I continued to listen, I was more disturbed by what I felt in my soul than I was by what he was saying. I could feel

> Paul prophesied...before there would be the revealing of the Anti-Christ, there would first be a "...Falling away" within the church.
>
> And you will notice a direct correlation between the End Time Apostasy and the rise of the False Teachers and False Prophets.

the influence of his words draw me into his twisted sense of logic. Listening to him made me feel like I needed to participate in this insane appeal he was presenting to his television audience. Deeply troubled by this I asked the Lord, "Why do I feel so moved by something that is so contrary to sound biblical truth and just plain common sense?" While wrestling with this in my mind I remembered a study I did several weeks before in Acts chapter 8 about the characteristics of Simon the Sorcerer. What began to be made obvious was that the spirit and presentation of this televangelist had the same characteristics as that of Simon the Sorcerer. They emanated from this man as he continued to speak.

SORCERY AND FALSE PROPHETS

It is the practice of sorcery that false prophets and false teachers have tapped into that enables them to influence the people that follow them. It is hard to resist if you listen long enough because the sorcerer operates in the realm of the spirit. When such an appeal is being made by someone with the spirit of sorcery to people who are in times of desperation, and overwhelmed by financial needs, discernment is easily overruled by need and the hope of a promising future. This is true if the promise is of a better financial future or just a better life free of pain and suffering.

The modern day sorcerer doesn't wear a turban and gaze into a crystal ball to reveal your future. No, they wear business suits, carry Bibles and use the name of God as they gaze into the television camera and prophesy your future, which is usually directly related to the size of the offering you send to their ministry.

DECEPTION AND MANIFESTATION GIFTS

I believe the nine manifestation gifts revealed in I Corinthians 12 are for today's church. I have ministered the gospel for more than 37 years. In my ministerial experience God has used all nine manifestation gifts to enable me to do the work He has called me to do. I cannot imagine doing the work of God without the precious gift of the Holy Spirit.

Over the years I have witnessed something that is quite disturbing to me. Manifestation gifts are often used in the realm of deception to validate one's ministry. I speak in Tongues; I Prophecy; I exercise Words of Knowledge and Words of Wisdom as the Spirit wills, but none of these manifestation gifts validate me or my doctrine. A manifestation gift is a gift given to the body of Christ for the profit of all, as Paul said in I Corinthians 12:7 (KJV) " But the manifestation of the Spirit is given to every man to profit withal".

The supernatural nature of a manifestation gift does not testify of who I am, but testifies of what Jesus did on the cross. Because a man or woman can prophecy or exercise other manifestation gifts, it does not mean they are people of godly character, nor does it validate their doctrine. I have said to audiences, "If you want to know what kind of man I really am, ask my wife and children". They will tell you!

> The modern day sorcerer doesn't wear a turban and gaze into a crystal ball to reveal your future. No, they wear business suits, carry Bibles and use the name of God as they gaze into the television camera and prophesy your future.

I have watched some who prophecy great mysteries about people's personal lives lead their followers into devastating doctrinal heresies. In Matthew 7:21-23 Jesus warned His disciples of the deceitful tendencies of those who "prophesy" and "...do many wonders". He said to His disciples, "Not everyone who says to Me, 'Lord, Lord,' shall enter the kingdom of heaven, but he who does the will of My Father in heaven. Many will say to Me in that day, 'Lord, Lord, have we not prophesied in Your name, cast out demons in Your name, and done many wonders in Your name?' And then I will declare to them, 'I never knew you; depart from Me, you who practice lawlessness

In verse 20 Jesus said, "Therefore by their fruits you will know them". "Fruit" speaks of character and anyone who would use the persuasive influence of the supernatural to coerce and ma-nipulate hurting and desperate people have a serious flaw in their character. And, we must remember, the devil offers a counter-feit for all nine gifts of the Holy Spirit mentioned in I Corinthians 12. Jesus said this would be a sign of the times.

According to John's gospel, chapter one, Jesus and the Word are one. Whoever you consider to be your spiritual leader, if he or she does not lead you to love and respect the Word of God, find another leader. As great as the ministry of prophecy and other manifestation gifts are to the church, it will never take the place of the ministry of the Word of God.

In Colossians 1:18 Paul said that, Christ...(the Word), was to have preeminence over all things that pertain to the church. The manifestation of prophecy and the written Word are not the same. The manifestation of prophecy is subjective, the written Word is authoritative, and Jesus said, *"Heaven and earth shall pass away, but my words shall not pass away"*.

Only Jesus!

Volumes can be written on this one subject, but we have neither the space nor time for an exhaustive study on false religion and its leaders, the false prophets. However, I will give you one basic truth that separates true religion from false religion. In Matthew 16:13 Jesus said to His disciples *"Who do men say that I the Son of man am?"* The disciples answered, *"Some say John the Baptist, some Elijah, and others Jeremiah or one of the prophets."* Then He said to them *"But who do you say that I am?"*

Peter answered, *"You are the Christ, the Son of the living God."* Peter's revelation of who Jesus was separates true religion from false religion. Who is Jesus? This is the question the whole world must answer. Who is Jesus? Not what church you go to, but who is Jesus? Jesus is the Christ the Son of the living God and the Savior of the world.

Every false religion can be identified by this one simple question. Who is Jesus? Whatever church you attend or whatever religion you may choose to be involved in, the absolute irrefutable truth that will keep you in right relationship with God is your answer to the question. Who is Jesus?

Beyond Religion

Deception in the last days will not be isolated to religion. Many of you reading this book have been victims of deception. You have been misled, lied to and deceived by those who have been very close to you, and now suffer the devastation of their evil, selfish ways.

A close friend of mine recently told me how he lost several million dollars in an investment scheme. What made this so difficult for him was that he met this "Investor" in church. Because he met the man in church, he let down his guard more easily than he would have otherwise.

I never thought I would live to see the day when so many leaders of the world would be so driven by deception. I am not talking about people who have made mistakes. I'm talking about those who have made lies and deceit a way of life.

I read a story one time about a Sunday school teacher who was teaching a class of fifth graders. The teacher asked the class, "Can anyone give me a definition of a lie?" The kids began shrugging their shoulders, looking at one another with blank faces. Finally, one young boy raised his hand. The teacher acknowledged him,

"Yes little John. Do you know the definition of a lie?" Little John responded, "Of course, a lie is a present help in a time of trouble." That's a cute answer for little John, but not so cute when it becomes one of the most common characteristics of leaders.

The headlines on the daily news are filled with revelations about lies and deceit in every level of government, the business world, and people's personal lives. The Bernie Madoffs have left their mark; and a wake of disaster has followed their evil deceptive business dealings. Part of the reason for the economical woes of this present time are founded in the lies and deceit of world leaders. Like little John, they use lies and deceit as a present help in times of trouble.

This, too, is a sign of the times Jesus spoke about. And as the analogy goes, the labor pains will continue to get worse and their frequency will increase as we see the day approaching. I caution you, do not allow the evil and deceitful ways of some lead you to cynicism.

There are evil people in the world, but there are also good people in the world. I have learned that you find what you look for in life. If you look for good people you will find them. If you look for deceivers, you will find them also. Keep your trust in Jesus. He is faithful, and as the scripture says in Proverbs 18:24, *"There is a friend who sticks closer than a brother,* and that friend is Jesus!

III. WARS AND RUMORS OF WARS

> [6] *"And you will hear of wars and rumors of wars. See that you are not troubled; for all these things must come to pass, but the end is not yet. For nation will rise against nation and kingdom against kingdom"*
>
> Matthew 24:6-7

The first three chapters of the book are about the wars of the

Apocalyptic Age. At the risk of being redundant, please allow me to reiterate a few thoughts that need to be repeated.

According to the words of Jesus there will be "Wars and Rumors of Wars." The words, *"See that you are not troubled"* are important. Notice it is a command. Jesus is saying, "There is something you must do when you see these things happening." The believer has a responsibility in the face of this worldwide crisis, *"See that you are not troubled!"* This is something you must do for yourself. Do not panic! Do not fear! Jesus did not say to pray that these wars will cease. He said, *"For all these things must come to pass, but the end is not yet!"* We hate war. God hates war. But wars will continue until the King of Kings and Lord of Lords rules and reigns in all the earth.

I am reminded of what Jesus said to His disciples in John 16:33, *"These things I have spoken to you, that in me you may have peace. In the world you will have tribulation; but be of good cheer, I have overcome the world."* Our peace is in knowing Him and in believing that He who gave His life for us has everything under control. For those of you who are like me, you wish there would never be another war. We will get what we hope for, but not yet! There will be more wars just as Jesus said there would be, *"For nation will rise against nation and kingdom against kingdom"* but be patient, for our day of peace is coming!

IV. FAMINES

> [7] *"...And there will be famines."*
>
> Matthew 24:7

It is not just by chance that Jesus followed His teaching on the subject of wars with the reality of famine. Notice the progression of the signs to this point in our study. Deception and the false prophets who propagate their lies are at the heart of wars. For example, there would be no "War on terror" as we know it, were it not for the false prophet Muhammad who prophesied to Islam that, "We must kill the infidels." This has been true throughout history. Wars are the result of people, nations and their leaders believing lies that have deceived them into thinking there must be a war.

> Jesus did not say to pray that these wars will cease. He said, *"For all these things must come to pass, but the end is not yet!"*

Deception – False Prophets – Wars – and Famine are all connected. The inevitable result of deception will be wars and the inevitable consequences of wars will be famine. This is why truth that comes by way of preaching the gospel must be done at any cost! Consequently, this is what has motivated me from the very beginning of my walk with God to obey the Great Commission and preach the gospel to every creature in every nation of the world. The message of the Gospel of the Kingdom of God is the only answer for a world that is filled with so much pain and suffering.

It is hard for those of us who live in the U.S. to identify with famine. Most of us dispose of more food than over two thirds of the world has to eat. I am going to share some statistics that are posted on the website "thinkquest.org."

In the Asian, African and Latin American countries, well over 500 million people are living in what the World Bank has called "absolute poverty,"

- Every year 15 million children die of hunger.

- For the price of one war missile, a school full of hungry children could eat lunch every day for 5 years.

- The World Health Organization estimates that one-third of the world is well fed, one-third of the world is under-fed and one-third is starving. In the time it takes to get on this website (thinkquest.org) at least 200 people have died of starvation.

- Nearly one in four people, 1.3 billion – a majority of humanity – live on less than $1 a day.

In the U.S. we have an epidemic of obesity. Two out of three adults are either overweight or obese. In addition, one out of every three children is either overweight or obese. Obesity in America is now adding an astounding $190 billion to the annual national healthcare price tag, exceeding smoking as public health enemy number one when it comes to cost. This is part of the reason why health care in America is so unaffordable."

In contrast to the obesity problem, America is hungry! One report estimated that one in every eight families in America is malnourished or hungry. One food relief agency, "Feeding America" is annually providing food to 37 million Americans, including 14 million children. "Feeding America's nationwide network of food banks is feeding 1 million more Americans each week than we did in 2006."

The hunger problem is greater than most people realize. It has the potential to cause one of the greatest crises this nation has ever known. Living on the Gulf Coast for most of my life we have become accustomed to preparing for hurricanes. When the National Oceanic Atmospheric Administration gives a hurricane warning for a certain area, we rush to the grocery stores to stock up on food. I am always amazed at how quickly the shelves become empty. Then near panic follows. As Americans we are used to going to our grocery store with the shelves filled to capacity with every grocery item the mind can imagine.

In 1991 I had the opportunity to minister in the nation of Romania for the first time. It was shortly after the longtime leader Nicolae Ceausescu was assassinated during a revolution which caused the fall of communism in that country in December of 1989. The country was in poverty and food was scarce. I will never forget the culture shock when I asked the missionary to take me to the grocery store. He said, "There are no grocery stores." Instead he took me to what he called a market. At the market, which was a facility that looked like an abandoned warehouse from the 1800's, there were vendors selling a variety of food items. Most of it was either undesirable or simply not fit to eat. It was a deplorable scene of poverty and desperation. After my first week in Romania, I lost 10 pounds and spent most of the time sick from eating the little food that was available.

When I returned to America after being there for almost a month, I wept when I walked into one of our grocery stores. Several weeks after I returned home from that country, a friend from Romania came to the U.S. to visit for the first time. When she got to America and walked into one of our grocery stores she too wept and said, "I did not know there was so much food in the whole world."

I believe the world and America are headed for a severe food shortage. How will Americans act when there is no food in our grocery stores? It will be the beginning of anarchy which will lead to Martial Law.

> The hunger problem is greater than most people realize. It has the potential to cause one of the greatest crises this nation has ever known.

This is a sobering reality we must consider. The America we have known for our lifetime is very quickly vanishing before our eyes. As we move toward socialism, we are losing our freedom in America. America is the proverbial "frog in the kettle" and we have already given up the option of jumping out of the water that is beginning to boil.

You may ask, "Do you really believe this can happen in America and the world before the Rapture of the Church?" Yes, I do, because of what I have already addressed in I Thessalonians 5:3. Let's look at it again, " *For when they say, 'Peace and safety!* *"'then sudden destruction comes upon them, as labor pains upon a pregnant woman.* **And they shall not escape**" (author's emphasis). Paul was speaking this message to the church, not to those who will be left behind for the Great Tribulation Period. In another writing I will deal more with preparation, but for now read the rest of I Thessalonians 5 and you will find an exhortation given by the Apostle Paul about what you must do to prepare for the days ahead.

Follow me as we continue to study this sobering reality. I know it is difficult to process the possibility of all these things in our heart and mind. But to ignore Jesus' teachings and the Apostle's ad-monition that they left behind for us would be totally irresponsible and would leave us unprepared for the things that are ahead. Before we move to the next point let me give you an encouraging word from Jesus in Luke 21:28, *"Now when these things begin to happen, look up and lift up your heads, because your redemption draws near."* Keep looking up no matter how challenging things may become because all these things tell us that the return of our Savior is near!

V. PESTILENCE

> 7 *"...pestilence..."*
>
> Matthew 24:7

Pestilence is defined as a contagious or infectious epidemic disease that is virulent and devastating. One of the Four Horsemen of the Apocalypse symbolizes plague or pestilence, placing the whole world on edge about pandemic outbreaks that threaten human existence. The H1N1 virus, Bird Flu, Swine Flu, Aids, Ebola, SARS are just a few of the possibilities. Experts believe a Bird Flu pandemic is imminent. Every year there seems to be a new strain of flu that threatens the world such as the ongoing West Nile Virus. Recent reports stated that 2012 was the worst year of West Nile in recorded history in the U.S.

The dengue virus, a deadly viral disease usually regarded as a risk only in the tropics, was recently found in a patient in Brownsville, Texas. Long thought to be eradicated in the U.S., scientists say dengue is roaring back as far north as New York and New Hampshire according to a 2009 report by the National Resource Defense Council. This virus also threatens a nationwide pandemic, and there is no known vaccine to protect against it or a medicine to cure it.

A pandemic is a disease affecting people over a wide geographical area and because of the transient nature of the world today this can happen in just a few days' time. I have always been amazed at how far you can travel in 24 or 36 hours by way of air bus. Consider, for example, an individual getting on an airplane with a deadly virus. The potential consequences to the other passengers and those at his final destination would be devastating and a pandemic forthcoming. The world has become a small place!

Not long ago a major news network had an article on whether a swine flu pandemic could result in a declaration of martial law in America and a suspension of constitutional rights. In the report it was estimated that this action would cause the following chain reaction: the closing of schools, closing the borders, forcibly quarantining and eliminating the right to freely assemble, preventing people from going to grocery stores and shopping malls. All these were mentioned as possibilities should these events occur.

The possibility of pandemic is nothing new to the world. Those familiar with the history of Europe will remember the Black Plaque of the 14th century. By the 1340's war was raging across the continent. Historians say it was a hundred year war. During this time the Mongol Empire of China established trade routes from Asia to Europe. But as the Mongols made the world a better place for business, they also planted the seed for its destruction.

Before 1347 the Mongols seemed unstoppable. Their dominion over the Middle East had lasted for nearly 150 years in an empire from the peaks of Tibet to the Volga River and from Beijing to Constantinople. Europe was greatly interested in the possibility of trade. What Europe did not know was that in the Far East an invisible death was sweeping across China, India and the Islamic world. These trade routes caused the pestilence to sweep across the continents and led to perhaps the greatest plague of all time "The Black Plague" of the 14th century.

Millions died in that medieval age. In some towns two-thirds of the population died from the black plague. The virus was air born and also carried by rodents from village to village. In just two years it spread from the Far East all the way to England, those were the days of the horse and buggy. In our modern world this could be replicated and spread worldwide in just 24 hours. Jesus said this would be a sign of the times.

VI. EARTHQUAKES

> 7"...and earthquakes in various places"
>
> Matthew 24:7

Another sign in the end times will be the increase of earthquakes. The NEIC (National Earthquake Information Center) reports there are about 20,000 earthquakes a year, or approximately 50 a day. Although the number of seismograph stations has increased over the years, many believe the frequency of quakes have and are continuing to increase.

Not many days go by without hearing about the latest scientific data that tells us California is due for "The Big One." In December 2004 the devastating tsunami that struck Indonesia was due to a sizable quake on the ocean floor and it killed thousands of people. Haiti is still trying to recover from the cataclysmic quake in January of 2010. More recently we all witnessed the horror of the ravaging, demolishing tsunami that hit Japan in 2011 which was also caused by an offshore earthquake. The tsunami that followed the quake in Japan led to one of the greatest nuclear disasters in history. This kind of news is so commonplace we have almost become numb to it. Jesus said this too is a sign of the times.

THE BEGINNING OF SORROWS

[8]*"All these are the beginning of sorrows."*
Matthew 24:8

In Matthew 24:8 Jesus said, *"All these are the beginning of sorrows."* Then He continued to describe more signs that would result in different kinds of troubles leading up to His return.

The remaining signs are of a different nature than the others we have dealt with. Persecution, offense and the absence of love are crimes of humanity, willful crimes that are the result of a people who have lost touch with the nature and character of their Creator.

VII. PERSECUTION

> [9] *"Then they will deliver you up to tribulation and kill you, and you will be hated by all nations for my names sake"*
>
> Matthew 24:9

The persecution of Christianity by the Romans and the Jews began as far back as the first century. To say Christianity has been persecuted for the past 2,000 years would be a gross understatement of the sufferings of millions since the crucifixion of Christ.

Persecution has not been limited to the first century. Persecution exists today across the world and that includes America. Below I will list only a few of the many statistics of persecuted Christians during the past 2,000 years.

- More than 43 million Christians have been murdered for their faith since the crucifixion of Jesus.

- It has been estimated that more Christians have been martyred for their faith in the 20th century than the prior 1,900 years combined.

- More than 200 million Christians in over 60 nations face persecution each day, 60% of these are children.

- 150,000 to 165,000 are martyred each year for their faith in Christ.

- These statistics continue to get worse each year.

Christians today are the most persecuted religious group in the world. This is mainly due to the rise of the radical Islamic agenda and the prevailing Anti-Christ spirit in the world. The top ten persecuting countries are: Burma/Myanmar, China, Egypt, Iran, Laos, North Korea, Pakistan, Saudi Arabia, Sudan (2 million since 1985), and Vietnam.

As we read these statistics, sadly, that's all they are to the average person, "statistics!" Somewhere in the world they represent some parent's child, some child's parents, a brother or sister, relative or friend. These numbers represent real people who lost their life simply because they believed that Jesus is the Son of God and the Savior of the world.

I remember a testimony told to me by a young man who escaped the oppression of the Romanian government in the late 80's, just a few years before communism was dismantled in that country. During the years of oppression the only religion that was recognized and permitted by the Romanian government was the Orthodox Church. This basically was a religion run by the government. There was the underground Protestant church and even Pentecostal churches but they were hidden from the mainstream public. Many were persecuted even unto death during this time if they were found practicing any religion besides the Orthodox state- run church.

In the midst of all this persecution there were many born again believers whose deep convictions would not allow them to be silent about their faith. This was evidenced when they had outdoor baptismal services in the local rivers and lakes. When they had these services the Romanian government would send spies to the place of meeting and take names and pictures of those being baptized. From that point on those who participated would be ostracized by the government and denied the necessary provisions that were provided to the people by them.

Some of these denials would prevent the young from receiving an education; or they might deny a man the right to work and make a living for his family. They might be denied medical care or some other necessary care that was all managed and provided by the government. What was so wonderful about those testimonies was that God would so transform their lives through the born again experience that they would choose to be baptized publicly no matter what the cost!

Persecution is coming to America. We are already beginning to feel the horrible results of this Anti-Christ spirit. How much will we have to endure before the rapture of the church is unknown, but know this,

> As we read these statistics, sadly, that's all they are to the average person...These numbers represent real people who lost their life simply because they believed that Jesus is the Son of God and the Savior of the world.

after the rapture occurs, the ultimate persecution of the church will begin when the Anti-Christ rules the entire world. The book of Revelation reveals this in great detail with the initiation of the "Mark of the Beast" during the Great Tribulation period. Those who refuse to receive the "Mark" will be subject to great difficulty, persecution and death.

VIII. OFFENSE

> [10] And then many will be offended, will betray one another, and will hate one another. [11] Then many false prophets will rise up and deceive many.
>
> Matthew 24:10-11

One may not think of offense as a sign of the time but Jesus said it would be one of the signs that would mark the beginning of the end. We live in a world that is relationally dysfunctional, and offense has a great part in this malady. This can easily be seen in the high divorce rate among American's and other world countries. It is also prevalent in the church of Jesus Christ. I have often wondered, "Why is it so difficult for people to get along?" The fact is we have all been offended and we are all guilty of offending someone else. Romans 3:23 says, *"for all have sinned and fall short of the glory of God,"*.

Have you noticed that the first four sins addressed in the Ten Commandments are sins against God. The last six address sins against man (man against man). In Matthew 18 Jesus strongly addressed the subject of offense and how to initiate reconciliation in verses 15-20.

> [15] *"Moreover if your brother sins against you, go and tell him his fault between you and him alone. If he hears you, you have gained your brother.* [16] *But if he will not hear, take with you one or two more, that 'by the mouth of two or three witnesses every word may be established.'* [17] *And if he refuses to hear them, tell it to the church. But if he refuses even to hear the church, let him be to you like a heathen and a tax collector.*
>
> [18] *"Assuredly, I say to you, whatever you bind on earth will be bound in heaven, and whatever you loose on earth will be loosed in heaven.*
>
> [19] *" Again I say to you that if two of you agree on earth concerning anything that they ask, it will be done for them by My Father in heaven.* [20] *For where two or three are gathered together in My name, I am there in the midst of them."*

We call this teaching the "Biblical Principles of Reconciliation" or the "The Matthew 18 Principle". Jesus followed this teaching with the parable of the "Unforgiving Servant". The parable is about one man who owed a debt to another man, accepting forgiveness for his debt, but refusing to do the same for the man who owed a debt to him. The parable illustrated what Jesus was saying to them in the principles of reconciliation. A careful study of this in Matthew chapter 18 is a must for every believer.

I have witnessed the devastating results of those who have committed offense and those who have been the victims of offense. Three things are true about offense:

1. We are all guilty of offending someone.

2. We have all been victims of the offense of someone else.

3. There is actual or real offense, and there is perceived offense.

Perceived Offense

Perceived offense is when someone interprets something to be offensive when it was never meant to be offensive. I see this in marriage relationships, parent – child, brother – sister, employee – employer, church leader – parishioner, and the list touches every relational aspect of our lives. Most of perceived offence could be avoided if we only did what Jesus said to do, *"…if your brother offend you go to your brother"*. I do not understand why this is so difficult.

Offense Leads to Deception

Notice what follows offense in Matthew 24:11, *"Then many false prophets will rise up and deceive many."* The word *"**Then**"* is significant. When people suffer offense, it makes them vulnerable to the deception of false teaching and false prophets. This is taking place in the present church world as I write.

Several years ago a significant number of people under my pastoral ministry got involved in one of the false religions sweeping through the church. And in almost every case, those who were drawn into this "new movement" experienced an offense or perceived offense that opened the door to the deception of the false religion.

The offense occurred between that person and someone else in the church, or their spouse, or some unrelated offense outside of their church involvement. As a result of the hurt from the unresolved offense they became vulnerable to the false doctrines of false prophets and false teachers. Jesus said this would be a sign of the times.

An offense, perceived or real causes a deep wound in the soul. When people are wounded they often do things they would not do otherwise. Sometimes their actions are completely irrational and make no sense to those around them.

OFFENSE – DECEPTION – APOSTASY

The consequences of these experiences are far reaching. I have already mentioned, it is the deception of the false prophets that lead to the apostasy of the end time church. In II Thessalonians 2:3 Paul warned the church about deception in light of the revealing of the Anti-Christ, *"Let no one deceive you by any means"*. He said the Anti-Christ would not be revealed until there would first be a falling away of the believer. This is the prophetic fulfillment of the apostasy in the End-Times. **The false prophets and false teachers are largely responsible for this apostasy with offenses setting the stage for many to be deceived by them in the end times.**

OFFENSE CREATES A PAINFUL VOID

Offense leaves a void inside each of us and depletes us of emotional energy, mental clarity, and sound judgment. Let me illustrate this on a familiar level, in the context of an intimate relationship between a man and woman, married or otherwise. When people break off a relationship with someone who has offended them, they will often jump into another relationship that makes no sense to those who know them and love them. Friends and family may shake their heads and say, "Why are they doing this? Why are they so blind?" Sometimes the newly found relationship is worse than the one they just left but the person involved can't see it. Men and women in troubled relationships have said to me, "She (He) caught me on the rebound; I was hurt, lonely and vulnerable."

The emotional hurt and pain from an unresolved conflict can be life shattering. A person who has been hurt by offense looks for love and acceptance and in their vulnerable state will accept it, even if it violates the truth's they held onto at one time. This is why Jesus said in Matthew 18:7 *"Woe to the world because of offenses! For offenses must come, but woe to that man by whom the offense comes."*

OFFENSE HAS DIVIDED THE CHURCH

I have spent much of my pastoral ministry in what we call the "Bible Belt" which includes the Appalachian mountainous area of the U.S. When my wife and I first moved into East Tennessee to begin our first church plant, we were amazed by the number of churches spread throughout the countryside. It seemed like no matter where you stood you could see a church somewhere on the side of the beautiful hills and mountains. We thought "Wow, this is awesome, churches are everywhere."

Later we learned the history of how these churches were started. Number one reason—division, the fruit of offense. One family gets into conflict with another family; people are offended and another church starts. One day one of the locals who had been around since the days of Noah's Ark... explained to me how this church started, and how that church started, and on and on. I finally asked him, **"Did any of these churches start on purpose?"** Sadly, it is documented by historical fact that most churches in these areas were started because someone was offended, and the outcome was a church split which led to another church.

OFFENSE IS A CHOICE

Remember, Jesus said this is a sign of the times, *"...many will be offended, will betray one another, and will hate one another."* Christian, please allow me to speak something meaningful into your life and for the sake of the Lord's church. You must deal with offense as you would a temptation. **In most cases you have to choose to be offended**. And most of the time we choose to take offense is because of pride and stubbornness in our hearts. We are too proud to admit we are wrong and too stubborn to do what Jesus taught us to do in Matthew 18, which is to release the one you feel owes you a debt. Give to them what God has given to you, forgiveness.

The Bible teaches that pride goes before a fall and that pride is at the root of an unforgiving spirit. I encourage you to read Matthew 18 very carefully. Meditate on it, study it and lay hold to the promise Jesus gave in the context in this teaching. He said, *"...where two or three are gathered together in My name, I am there in the midst of them."* Jesus gave us this promise in the context of reconciling broken relationships that are the result of offense (Matthew 18:7, 20). Conflict, strife, betrayal and bitterness are the fruits of offense. Jesus promised that when we resolve conflict the way He instructed, He will be there to help.

Oh, how I long to see the church become loving and forgiving which is the true Spirit of Christ. Jesus prayed to His Father in John 17:21-23, *"That they all may be one, as You, Father, are in Me, and I in you; that they also may be one in Us, that the world may believe that You sent Me."* There is no doubt, the greatest thing we can do for ourselves and the Kingdom of God is to love, forgive and learn how to handle offense in a biblical way. The motivation to do so is strong, as Jesus said *"...that the world may believe that You have sent Me."* That is a strong admonition to do it the way Jesus said to do it.

Because this problem is so prevalent in our world I find it difficult to find a stopping point here. However, I will say a final word.

We all have our place in the fulfillment of prophecy. The question is, "What part of the prophetic future are you fulfilling?" Of the many prophecies given to us in God's word, which one bears your name? Will you be numbered with the apostates in the End-Time? Will you be a victim of offense and choose to follow a false religion? Or perhaps you have become like the third person in the parable of the talents, who has become so withdrawn by offense that you have hidden your talent from fruitful use for the Kingdom of God because you are too offended to exercise it to His glory.

My hope and prayer is that you will be numbered with the overcomers. That you will choose to persevere through every temptation and obstacle that Satan puts in your path. That you will continue to be a witness until that glorious day when our Savior appears in the clouds to take us home for the great reunion of the Saints of God, and the Marriage Supper of the Lamb of God. Believe me Friend, *" For I consider that the sufferings of this present time are not worthy to be compared with the glory which shall be revealed in us"* (Romans 8:18). You do not want to miss that great day because someone has offended you. Press on! I will be looking for you on that great day!

IX. FALSE PROPHETS (DISCUSSED IN SUBTOPIC II DECEPTION)

X. THE ABSENCE OF LOVE

> [12] *"And because lawlessness will abound, the love of many will grow cold"*
>
> Matthew 24:12

There is an exponential increase in lawlessness or as the KJV says "Iniquity" in the world today. Immorality, shamelessness, rebellion against God and a casting off of moral restraint will characterize the last days.

I didn't know the Lord when I was a teen, and as many others in my day, I got involved in the party scene of drugs, alcohol and the moral collapse of the sexual revolution that marked the 60's and 70's. I was considered a rebellious teen with little regard for authority. Had the Lord not saved me and changed my life at age 19, I probably would have not lived to see my 25th birthday. I was on a fast track to a devil's hell.

I recently saw a news program about the much celebrated annual event in the U.S. known by our college students as "Spring Break." The debauchery of this annual event makes the rebellion of my youth look like child's play. The profound difference in the rebellion of my generation and that of present times is this: What we did behind closed doors, this generation not only does in public, but shamelessly before cameras that circulate their debauchery all across the world. Sexual perversion, adultery, fornication, homosexuality, drugs, drunkenness, lustful entertainment, nudity, all happen in the name of "Party" or "having a good time".

What is really astounding to me is that this annual event is financed by the parents of these college age young people. Mom and Dad, what on earth is going on in your mind when you finance a spring break event for your child? The statistics of those who are injured or die at these events are staggering. A few years ago over 20 young people died during spring break in Panama City, Florida. Then there are the literal thousands who will contract a sexually transmitted disease (STD) they will have to live with for the rest of their lives, or those who will become pregnant, followed by their first abortion.

What might seem to be a cultural event to this generation is a sign of the times. Jesus said, *"As it was in the days of Noah…as it was also in the days of Lot."* God destroyed the earth with a flood because the world had become so sinful in Noah's day. He destroyed Sodom and Gomorrah with fire and brimstone because of their immorality and sexual perversion. If God did not put a stop to all this, He would have to repent for the flood in Noah's day and raise Sodom and Gomorrah. He will not repent for the flood and He will not raise Sodom and Gomorrah; however, He will destroy all those who choose to live such sinful and rebellious lifestyles, *"shall have their part in the lake which burns with fire and brimstone, which is the second death"* (Revelation 21:8).

The Absence of Love

Jesus said, *"the love of many will grow cold."* The continued practice of lawlessness will produce an entire generation of people that do not know what it means to love. I mean **real love**, not the imitation love that is being pawned off on our generation. The Bible says *"God is Love"*. When people choose to live life without

God, they separate themselves from the only source of real love there is in the world. The absence of this love causes a deep gaping hole inside a person's soul. The immorality and sexual perversion of this generation is an attempt to fill this void with sinful practices. However, the more you try to fill the emptiness of your soul with sin the more empty you will be!

We live in a loveless world. The apostle Paul said this would be characteristic of the apostasy of the end times (II Timothy 3:1-4). *"But know this, that in the last days perilous times will come:*

> The profound difference in the rebellion of my generation and that of present times is this: What we did behind closed doors, this generation not only does in public, but shamelessly before cameras that circulate their debauchery all across the world.

For men will be lovers of themselves, lovers of money...lovers of pleasure rather than lovers of God."

All these signs and more will be like distress flags waving in the hands of our Savior trying to get our attention warning us that the end is near. Do you see the flags? Do you see our loving Savior on the shores of eternity trying to get your attention? Jesus is about to return, the rapture of the church is closer than you may think!

X. A PROMISE AND THE MANDATE OF THE CHURCH

THE PROMISE

[13] *"But he who endures to the end shall be saved"*

Matthew 24:13

Jesus said that if we would endure we would be saved. The word endure means to persevere; keep on keeping on; don't quit;

do not stop; be faithful until the end! According to the promise of God you will be saved from the cataclysmic events that will take place during the Great Tribulation.

My heart is often broken when I see so many who at one time had a passion for God, but over time has drawn back into complacency and a compromised lifestyle. It has been said, "It's not how you start, but how you finish." Far too many have a testimony about an experience they had at some point in the past, but have no reality of God in their life today, simply because they did not continue to endure the many trials and temptations of this present world.

Dear Friend, if you are one that has drawn back and are not living the life you have been called to, you still have time to make things right. Don't waste any time. Do not put it off another day. Call on the Lord before you read another word, and God will hear you, forgive you and set you on a path that will not only lead to your salvation but also your family and many around you.

The Mandate of the Church

> [14] *"And this gospel of the kingdom will be preached in all the world as a witness to all the nations, and then the end will come"*
>
> Matthew 24:14)

The End Time church has a mission, and that mission is to do everything we can to take "...*this gospel of the kingdom*" to the ends of the earth. An important key to that mission is found in the words "...*this gospel of the kingdom.*" In the context of what Jesus was teaching there can be no mistake about how we should invest our time, energy and finances, especially as we see the day approaching. Sharing the message of His return is the first and chief thing we must do in the days that remain.

There are many messages circulating around the church today but they are not *"...this gospel of the kingdom."* I hear the self-help guru's teaching the church how to be successful and prosperous. Too much is about being successful in the now and not enough about the soon coming return of our Lord. Many are going to leave behind great wealth for the Anti-Christ and have precious little in the life to come. Truly, *"the first shall be last and the last shall be first."* Some are so consumed with the success of this world, it has become a snare to them, and many will be left behind with all their wealth that will be turned into rubbish in a few moments' time.

> My heart is often broken when I see so many who at one time had a passion for God, but over time has drawn back into complacency and a compromised lifestyle. It has been said, "It's not how you start, but how you finish."

Doomsday Preppers

Not long ago the National Geographic Channel began a series called "Doomsday Preppers." The program is about people all over the world, but mainly in the United States who are going to extreme measures to prepare for the cataclysmic events of the near future or as some say, "The Apocalypse". They are stockpiling food and water, arming themselves with guns and large amounts of ammo. They have escape plans and what they call a "Bug out Plan" for when the expected chaos begins. Their plan is to take their families to a safe place in some remote facility where they hope to survive the meltdown of society and the approaching apocalypse.

Some with more financial resources have purchased large tracks of land in remote places where several families have committed to defending their fortress and living off the land. It has become a multi-million dollar business for fabrication shops that are building steel constructed apartments that are being buried under ground or placed in the sides of mountains. One family purchased a former ICBM missile silo from the government and has turned it into an underground apartment and bomb shelter.

Some of these people are former military personnel who have recently returned from war in Iraq or Afghanistan. Their wartime experiences have enlightened them to the devastation of society when anarchy breaks out and governments collapse. As soldiers fighting in a war they have witnessed firsthand the inhuman things people will do in desperation to survive.

I have watched several of these programs and found a number of things of interest.

1. Many of these people are plain ordinary everyday people. Some were educated professionals with families that live normal lives.

2. Their preparation is motivated by different fears about the future, such as:

   - A nuclear holocaust
   - Anarchy
   - Famine
   - Pandemic
   - Economical collapse
   - Polar shifts
   - War
   - Earthquakes
   - Tidal rise
   - Volcanic eruption

   And more

3. Perhaps the most amazing thing is that they do not profess to be Bible-believing Christians who have been

schooled in the teachings of Eschatology. They are not being motivated by religious beliefs.

Amazingly, all of the catastrophic events they fear will happen in the near future, according to Bible Prophecy and can be found in the study of the "Signs of the Times" in Matthew 24 and in other New Testament Epistles. The "Doomsday Preppers" sense something in their soul telling them the world is in trouble. They know things are not right. They know something fearful is about to happen; they know this not because of religious beliefs but instinctively! Furthermore, they are so sure of what they believe about the near future, they are taking extreme measures to prepare themselves and their families for what is ahead.

The question to us is this: Should we dismiss them as doomsday fanatics or should we take their concerns seriously?

Another group of people we cannot ignore are modern day scientists. Scientists are also warning the world of a cataclysmic future. Scientists as well as Doomsday Preppers are warning us about the same things found in the biblical study of the "Signs of the Times. Their warnings are purely from a scientific perspective, not some fearful concern in their soul like the Preppers.

HURRICANE KATRINA

The disaster caused by Hurricane Katrina on August 29, 2005 was considered the worst natural disaster in United States history. The official death toll, according to the Louisiana Department of Health, was 1,464 people. This hurricane cost the Gulf Coast region an estimated $125 Billion dollars. The aftermath caused the labor force to diminish and wages to decrease by staggering amounts. Between July 2005 and July 2007, there was an estimated loss of 70,000 jobs as a result of the hurricane.

The real tragedy is that much of the loss could have been avoided if we had taken seriously the warnings given for more than a decade before. Dr. Ivor van Heerden, Ph.D., holds a doctorate degree in Marine Sciences and was the deputy director of the Louisiana State University (LSU) Hurricane Center, before being dismissed by LSU following Hurricane Katrina. Dr. Heerden warned of the possible scenario of such a disaster years before Katrina hit in 2005.

This is one case in our lifetime when God tried to use scientists to warn us about a cataclysmic event but no one would listen. The problems with such warnings are that they are not taken seriously, or we think we have more time to prepare than we actually do. Tomorrow always seems to be a better time to prepare than today!

IS GOD TRYING TO GET OUR ATTENTION?

Not many days will go by without someone questioning me with great concern and sincerity about what is happening on a global level. What does it mean? **God is trying to get our attention!** History proves that the Lord will not leave things the way they are and He will not do anything without revealing His secrets to His prophets (Amos 3:7).

Historically, when something of a broad cataclysmic nature was about to erupt, God not only spoke to the prophets but also pagans such as in the days of the rule of the Pharaoh's in ancient Egypt. In Genesis chapter 41 we have the Biblical account of when Pharaoh the ruler of Egypt was disturbed by a dream. The dream was a mystery to Pharaoh and one that greatly disturbed him. He did not understand the dream until Joseph the son of Israel gave him the interpretation by way of revelation from God.

Pharaoh's dream was about a drought followed by famine that would come upon the land after seven years of a bountiful harvest. As Joseph interpreted the dream to Pharaoh, **God gave him wisdom to know how to prepare the people and ultimately spare their lives through the drought.**

In like manner God is doing the same thing today. He is moving upon people such as the Preppers, scientist and others, revealing to them that the end of human existence as we know it is near. Their fear is genuine, the problem, like in the days of ancient Egypt God has given His covenant people insight about how to prepare for what is ahead, but… unlike Pharaoh, today's world leaders refuse the hear. Isn't it sad… even an idol worshiper like Pharaoh listened to the man of God and gave place to his wisdom, but our proud educated world will not hear! And sadly much of the church is doing the same!

Please listen my Friend, God is trying to get our attention. The Spirit of Joseph is in the land. God gave Joseph a revelation about Pharaohs dream which spared the life of an entire nation. The church of Jesus Christ has a revelation of future events. Scientist are giving their warnings. And people just instinctly know something of a cataclysmic nature is just over the horizon.

God will not allow His creation to walk head on into the devastating things facing us in the near future without giving us a message for survival. Do not turn a deaf ear to what the Lord is trying to make real to your soul. As I have already encouraged you numerous times thus far, call upon the Lord, He will hear you and help you to be prepared for what is about to take place.

What shall we do in the light of all these things? In Luke 12:40 Jesus said: *"Be ye therefore ready also: for the Son of man cometh at an hour when ye think not"* (KJV).

The Unexpected Return

Chapter 6

In this chapter we will look at a repeating theme centered on the return of Christ, **"He will come in an unexpected time."** Jesus referred to this constantly as He taught about the Signs of the Times, the Rapture, the Great Tribulation and His Second Coming.

One of the first things I want to establish from a sound systematic study of the Bible is that **"No one knows the day and hour of His return!"** I've watched many people make fools of themselves along with the people who follow them as they have attempted to predict the exact time of Jesus' return. If you were to search the internet, you would find many resources, articles and books written on the latest revelation from someone who has figured out the time of His return. **Do not give them the time of day!**

I understand there is something within man that wants to know the "When?" I think it started when we were kids traveling with our parents, "when will we get there, how long will it take, are we there yet?" As children we were the perpetrators of this crime and as parents we become the victims.

In Acts 1:6 the last question the disciples had for Jesus before His ascension was *"…will you at this time restore the kingdom to Israel?"* In other words, are we there yet? Because Jesus built up such great expectation about His kingdom the only thing on their mind was, "are we there yet, does it begin now?" The Olivet Discourse started the same way. After Jesus prophesied the destruction of the temple the next question was *"…Tell us, when shall these things be?"* In the Olivet Discourse He completely ignored their question and proceeded to teach about His second coming and the signs of the times. In Acts 1:7 He said to them, *"And he said unto them, It is not for you to know the times or the seasons, which the Father hath put in His own power"* (KJV).

In everyday plain English "Jesus blew them off" both times! Knowing the inherit nature of man and his desire to know "when", Jesus repeatedly said in His teaching of the Rapture that no one would know the day and hour of His return. Let us look at several scriptures that verify that.

> [36] *"But of that day and hour no man knows, not even the angels of heaven, but my Father only."*
> Matthew 24:36

> [42] *"Watch therefore, for you do not know what hour your Lord is coming."*
> Matthew 24:42

> [44] *"Therefore you also be ready, for the Son of man is coming at an hour you do not expect."*
> Matthew 24:44

> [13] *"Watch therefore, for you know neither the day nor the hour in which the Son of Man is coming."*
> Matthew 25:13

In Mark 13:32 Jesus said *"But of that day and hour no one knows, not even the angels in heaven, nor the Son, but only the Father."*

Of course, we understand that when Jesus said, not even the Son knows the time, He was making reference to the willful limitations He subjected Himself to in His earthly ministry. We see this in the book of Philippians chapter two in what is called the Kenosis of Christ, which teaches us that Jesus set aside His God-like attributes and took upon Himself the form of a man. Jesus was the God/Man in His earthly ministry.

The Apostle Paul would extend this attitude to the Epistles about the "When" question after he gave us the theology for the Rapture. In I Thessalonians 5:1-2 Paul drew attention away from the "when" question. I can almost feel the unspoken thoughts of the apostle. It is as though he knew after he gave the detailed description about the Rapture (I Thessalonians 4:13-18) that their first thought would be "When?" So before he continued on the subject he said, *"But concerning the times and the seasons, brethren, you have no need that I should write to you."*

A THIEF IN THE NIGHT

Then he said something that laid the foundation for what really mattered. *"For you yourselves know perfectly that the day of the Lord comes as a thief in the night."* Now we have a foundation to build on. Another metaphor or word picture he used likened the coming of the Lord to a thief in the night.

Jesus also used this metaphor in Matthew 24:40-44 after He gave a vivid illustration of what will happen when the Rapture takes place, *"Then two men shall be in the field: one shall be taken and the other left. Two women will be grinding at the mill: one will be taken and the other left. Watch therefore, for you do not know what hour your Lord is coming."*

We will study these scriptures later, but His message is consistent and unmistakable. God has not and will not reveal to man the exact day and hour of His return. Many have wasted their time on this subject and have missed the more important part of this message: To direct your passion and energy in preparation for this great event, not try to figure out when it will happen.

Remember this truth: Do not spend time trying to see things that are not clearly revealed. And when someone claims to have an exclusive revelation everyone else does not have, that is the first warning that it is not of God.

HE TOLD US TO WATCH

Jesus gave important instruction concerning the **unexpected return of Christ.** He summed it up with two thoughts, a word and a word picture. **First,** the word "Watch."

God HAS NOT and WILL NOT reveal to man the exact day and hour of His return.

Second, the word picture, "...if the master of the house had known what hour the thief would come, he would have 'watched' and not allowed his house to be broken into" (Matthew 24:43)

Let us take a look at the word **"Watch."** It is used four times in the Olivet Discourse. Three times the word is a verb and once a noun. There is something of great value to be learned by the use of this one word concerning our readiness or preparedness as we look to the **unexpected return of the Lord.**

The verb, the Greek word, *gregoreuo*, has the meaning of - keeping awake, to be watchful, be vigilant and spiritual alertness.

The noun, the Greek word, *phulake* , is used as the act of a person in a certain place, a guard standing his post, a sentinel. It is the same word used in Luke 2:8 which gives interesting insight about what Jesus was trying to teach His disciples. Let's go to the book of Luke and take a look at this story.

> *8"Now there were in the same country shepherds living out in the fields, keeping **watch** over their flock by night.*
> *9 And behold, an angel of the Lord stood before them, and the glory of the Lord shone around them, and they were greatly afraid.*
> *10 Then the angel said to them, do not be afraid, for behold, I bring you good tidings of great joy which will be to all people.*
> *11 For there is born to you this day in the city of David a Savior, who is Christ the Lord."*
>
> Luke 2:8-11 (emphasis author's)

I find it interesting that Jesus used the same Greek word to prepare His disciples for His second coming as was used in the Biblical account of when the angels announced His first coming.

WHAT DOES IT MEAN TO US?

There is no deep hidden message in what Jesus was saying to His disciples 2,000 years ago, or to those of us who are preparing for and looking for His return today. The message is simple. **"Strive to maintain a close spiritual walk with the Lord and be diligent to 'watch' over what He has given you and called you to do."** I want to spend a little time on this thought. It is a very important point in our study and I want to be sure you understand it.

1. **Your Spiritual Walk** - It is the God-given responsibility of every believer to maintain the disciplines of a spiritual

life. Your relationship with God is a personal walk with you and the Lord. Others can help you with your walk but no one can do it for you. Just like any relationship there are some basic disciplines that you must apply.

It begins with a decision to follow Christ. Christ gives you an invitation; then it's your choice to follow Him. There are some basic teachings in scripture that lay a foundation for anyone who desires to follow Christ. It is not my objective to write on personal discipleship at this point, but I encourage the reader to learn what it means to be a true disciple of Christ. I will give you just a few foundational thoughts, you need a church, a Pastor, a Bible, and you must learn to pray which simply means learning to talk to God in a deep personal and meaningful way. And put God first in your life above all else, *"But seek first the kingdom of God and His righteousness, and all these things shall be added to you"* (Matthew 6:33 NKJV).

2. **Watch –** I do not know of a better word picture than that of the shepherds in the field watching over their flock when the angels announced the birth of Jesus. It brings to mind the nativity scene that is such a big part of decorating our homes for Christmas.

The message: The shepherds were watching over what God had given them to care for, and for them it was sheep. This far reaching message speaks to us in every dimension of our life. The relationship of a shepherd and his sheep is very personal. The life of the sheep is dependent on the loving care

> Strive to maintain a close spiritual walk with the Lord and be diligent to 'watch' over what He has given you and called you to do.

of a good shepherd. Jesus identified Himself as a shepherd to His disciples. In John 10:11, Jesus said *"I am the good shepherd; the good shepherd gives his life for the sheep."*

To "**watch**" has the connotation of a spiritual man or woman taking care of what God has given them to do in life. Not just doing it in a mechanical way. When a person has a genuine relationship with God, they lovingly care for what God has given him or her, and anxiously await the return of the Lord. Are you being a good shepherd over what God has given you?

A Thief

Jesus was a master communicator. He was recognized by Nicodemus the ruler of the Jews as, *"...a teacher from God."* To further illustrate to His disciples what it meant to be watchful, He used the word picture of a thief and followed with three parables. We will look at each one and allow God to speak to us by way of the words of our Savior. This will help us have a better understanding of this important message of our Lord and that we may learn what it means to be watchful.

How strange that Jesus would use the word picture of a thief to communicate a message to His disciples. Why a thief? What was Jesus trying to say? The first thing that comes to my mind when I think of a thief is "Loss." What will he take? What valuable items do I have in my home that a thief might take and I'd never see again?

The conclusive thought is that "if I do not watch I may lose something of Great value." **In the context of what Jesus was teaching it could only refer to one thing of great value and that is the Rapture of the church.** The repeated message of watching and being vigilant is for the purpose of not missing the Rapture of the church. In Luke 21:36 Jesus summed it up with these words.

*"Watch therefore, and pray always that you may be counted worthy to **escape** all these things that will come to pass and to stand before the Son of Man."*

The **escape** is the Rapture. Some people do not like the idea of escape or as some call it **"escapism theology"**, but that's too bad because it was Jesus' idea. It is His will that we escape the things that are coming upon the earth because as Paul said in, I Thessalonians 5:9, *"For God did not appoint us to wrath, but to obtain salvation through our Lord Jesus Christ."* It is not the will of God that His precious sheep suffer the devastation that is coming upon the world during the Great Tribulation Period.

Three Parables

The master teacher did not stop here because this is such an important subject concerning end time events. He didn't want His message to be misunderstood. Therefore, He followed with the teaching of three parables. It is worth noting that He told these parables in the Olivet Discourse between the teaching of the Signs of the Times and the Judgment of the Nations. Let's take a look at the message.

FIRST PARABLE: THE FAITHFUL AND WISE SERVANT

45Who then is a faithful and wise servant, whom his master made ruler over his household, to give them food in due season? 46 Blessed is that servant whom his master, when he comes, will find so doing. 47 Assuredly, I say to you that he will make him ruler over all his goods. 48 But if that evil servant says in his heart, 'My master is delaying his coming,' 49 and begins to beat his fellow servants, and to eat and drink with the drunkards, 50 the master of that servant will come on a day when he is not looking for him and at an hour that he is not aware of, 51 and will cut him in two and appoint him his portion with the hypocrites. There shall be weeping and gnashing of teeth.

Matthew 24:45-51

He began with a question, *"Who then is a faithful and wise servant, whom his master made ruler over his household, to give them food in due season?"* Who is Jesus speaking to? First of all the parable is a continuation of what He had already said as recorded in Matthew 24:1-44, but now He is creating another word picture. He is building upon what He has already spoken for greater clarification of the message He wants to communicate.

THREE KEY WORDS FROM THE PARABLE:

- ▸ 1 - Faithful
- ▸ 2 - Wise
- ▸ 3 - Servant

I can't help but think about pastoral ministry when I read these words. Every pastor and true servant of God should be **faithful, wise and have a servant's heart**. I believe He is first of all speaking to those of us who have been given responsibilities as leaders in the church because of the words, *"...whom his master has made ruler over his household, to give them food in due season."* These words speak directly to those who have been called to Pastor the Church of God.

It makes me think of Jesus' encounter with Peter after His resurrection. You can find this story in John's gospel chapter 21. Peter, still struggling with the fact that he had denied his Lord three times, finds Jesus on the sea shore. Jesus never confronted Peter about his denial, but He did confront him about his responsibility as a leader in the church. Jesus prepared breakfast for Peter and after they ate He asked Peter if he loved Him. Most of you are familiar with the story; if you are not I encourage you to stop here and read it for yourself in John chapter 21.

Three times Jesus asked Peter if he loved Him, three times Peter responded," yes" and three times Jesus said *"Feed my sheep."* Jesus was talking about people, not the cute little woolly creatures in the farm yard. Feeding the sheep is the responsibility of the pastor and leaders of the local church as well as the responsibility of parents to their children. Our God-given responsibility is to feed them which speaks of spiritual food not the food we eat at the dinner table.

Jesus goes on to say, *"Blessed is that servant whom his master, when he comes, will find doing."* (Matthew 24:46)

A friend of mine Pastor Paul Wilde recently wrote a book titled "Smitten Shepherds." In his book he shares some startling statistics about pastoral ministry over the past several years. Approximately 1,500 pastors a month are resigning pastoral ministry in the U.S. That is 18,000 a year (updates show that number has increased). I will not get into the many and varied reasons why this is so, but it is a travesty in the modern day church. **Many have forgotten what Jesus said, we are to be "Faithful and Wise Servants" until the very end. The message is *"But he that shall endure unto the end, the same shall be saved"* (Matthew 24:13 KJV)**

He blesses the servant that continues to do what he has been called to do and promises to *"make*

> Jesus goes on to say, *"Blessed is that servant whom his master, when he comes, will find doing."* Matthew 24:46

him ruler over all his goods," which I believe is the reward of ruling and reigning with Christ in the Millennial Kingdom. Jesus had strong words of condemnation to those who refused to fulfill their responsibility to take care of the house of God as we prepare for the return of the Lord.

This message is not limited to the calling of pastoral ministry. The parable also challenges every man and woman to be spiritual leaders of their home. **Mom and Dad, the greatest responsibility you have as a parent is to pass your faith on to your children.** Do not let education, sports, recreation or anything else; become more important than your child learning about who Jesus is and His soon coming return. The message of the parable is simple, be faithful, be wise and be a servant until the return of the Lord. Watch over your house pastor, parent, and if you do you will share and have your part as a ruler in the greatest Kingdom the world has ever known.

I want to address a personal word to the pastors and church leaders and then I will address the parents with something I feel strongly impressed by the Spirit of God to say to you.

Pastors

Of the 37 years and counting that I have been involved in ministry I have served as a senior pastor for 29 of those years. I love pastoral ministry as revealed in scripture. I have the calling for it and with that calling is the grace to serve in that capacity. What I do not like is the cultural Americanized version of the pastor. American culture has adulterated the Biblical mandate of what a pastor is supposed to be, and in many cases have made him a "Hireling."

I can sympathize, although not agree, with the large number

of pastors resigning from pastoral ministry. **The American version of pastoral ministry and the expectations that come with it are the single greatest contributor to so many who have left their calling in pursuit of some other profession.** The problem is not the expectation of the Biblical description of what a pastor should be, but the American cultural expectation of what people believe a pastor should be.

Pastor, remember this, your primary responsibility is to do what Jesus told Peter to do, "Feed My sheep." This is the first and foremost responsibility that is given to you by God. Therefore, because of your calling you have grace to do this, but all this other **"stuff"** that has been put on us by a culture that has been born out of narcissism and secular humanism will destroy the gift and calling of God in your life.

> Pastors, your primary responsibility is to do what Jesus told Peter to do, "Feed My sheep."

Do what Jesus said to do and God will honor you. Remember what Jesus said to His disciples as He sent them out, " *And whoever will not receive you nor hear your words, when you depart from that house or city, shake off the dust from your feet"* (Matthew 10:14). God is with you and will give you the grace you need to do what He has called you to do. **And, if you are truly called of God to preach this great message, when He returns He needs to find you doing so!** If you are not, you will not be numbered with the faithful and wise servants Jesus spoke about. Pastor, this parable is about you!

PARENTS

Parents, you have been given an awesome responsibility by God to *"Train up a child in the way he should go:* (Proverbs 22:6

KJV). **Dads, it is your responsibility to see to it that your child has the opportunity to find Jesus as their savior.** You may become the most successful man among your professional peers but if your children do not have the opportunity to know Jesus, you have failed as a man and a father.

Notice I carefully use the word **"Opportunity"**, because you cannot save them; you can only create an environment for them to have the opportunity to know Him. Knowing Jesus will be their choice. I realize some of you mothers do not have the father of your children to help you and this awesome responsibility has fallen solely upon you.

One of the greatest burdens I have in pastoral ministry is for the many single parents raising children without the help of the other. In some cases, because of an early untimely death, the father or mother has passed on. All too often, it is a failed marriage that has resulted in abandonment. Then there is only one parent left to struggle with the burden of trying to be both parents.

Mom, Dad, I know the demand upon you in today's world of American culture. Time is sacred, however, you must make time to pray with your children and take them to church. I always enjoyed reading a Bible story to my children before bedtime followed with a prayer. I was always astonished at how many things a child wants you to pray for: the dog, the cat, the friend at school or the friend's sick grandmother 1,000 miles away, precious moments in parenting which can never be replaced with any other activity.

As a pastor so often I wish parents would take the spiritual needs of the child as seriously as the soccer game or baseball game, or dance team and the many other activities that our American culture has told us we cannot live without.

Parents, Children and the Rapture

I have already addressed this in chapter 4, but I want to say one final word to the parent regarding you, your child and the Rapture of the church. The child will never have more faith and commitment to God than you the parent. Will you go in the Rapture? The greater question, will your children go in the Rapture? You have a bigger part in this than you may think. It is rare, if nearly impossible, for a child to have a greater faith than the parent. As goes the parent, so goes the child. If you don't make it, it is very unlikely your children will make it. Be a faithful and wise servant and you and your children will be spared all the horrible things that will come upon the earth during the Great Tribulation Period!

> Will you go in the Rapture? The greater question, will your children go in the Rapture?.....As goes the parent, so goes the child. If you don't make it, it is very unlikely your children will make it.

Moms and Dads this is something you need to give some very serious thought to. I encourage you to read the book of Revelation. As you do take special note of the many horrid things that are coming upon the world as the Apocalypse begins to unfold. No parent that loves their children wants them to be left behind for the suffering, persecution, plague, disease, hunger, nuclear holocaust and more that will come upon this earth. If you can't find the motivation to be prepared for yourself, consider your children. For their sake you must do what needs to be done to be prepared for that unexpected return of our Lord.

If you and your family are not a part of a local church you have an assignment, "Find one!" In Hebrews 10:25 the writer says *"not forsaking the assembling of ourselves together, as is the man-*

ner of some, but exhorting one another, and so much the more as you see the day approaching." Notice the words "...so much the more as you see the day approaching." As the day of the Lord draws near we should be more involved with the local church than ever before.

Finding a good church is like anything else. It takes time, effort, and a prayerful heart. And when you find a church be a giver, not just one who takes. Be an encourager, not a complainer. I have learned that you find what you look for in life. If you look for the right things you will find them!

SECOND PARABLE: THE TEN VIRGINS

> [1] *"Then the kingdom of heaven shall be likened to ten virgins who took their lamps and went out to meet the bridegroom.* [2] *Now five of them were wise, and five were foolish.* [3] *Those who were foolish took their lamps and took no oil with them,* [4] *but the wise took oil in their vessels with their lamps.* [5] *But while the bridegroom was delayed, they all slumbered and slept.*

> [6] *"And at midnight a cry was heard: 'Behold, the bridegroom is coming; go out to meet him!'* [7] *Then all those virgins arose and trimmed their lamps.* [8] *And the foolish said to the wise, 'Give us some of your oil, for our lamps are going out.'* [9] *But the wise answered, saying, 'No, lest there should not be enough for us and you; but go rather to those who sell, and buy for yourselves.'* [10] *And while they went to buy, the bridegroom came, and those who were ready went in with him to the wedding; and the door was shut.*

> [11] *"Afterward the other virgins came also, saying,*

'Lord, Lord, open to us!' [12] *But he answered and said, 'Assuredly, I say to you, I do not know you.'*

[13] *"Watch therefore, for you know neither the day nor the hour in which the Son of Man is coming.*

Matthew 25:1-13

Once again Jesus, the master teacher continues His exhortation to be watchful. Like the Rabbis of His time Jesus used simple word pictures to communicate His thoughts to the world, then and now. This was Jesus' most common way of teaching. His stories appealed to the young and old, the rich and poor, the educated and simple. Consider this: He reached out to uneducated people like the fishermen He called to be disciples, who later became the great Apostles of the New Testament.

In this particular parable He likened the kingdom of heaven to *"ten virgins, which took their lamps, and went forth to meet the bridegroom."* Every word of symbolism in this story has an important meaning in reference to being prepared for the Lord's return.

The message is enlightening, encouraging and sobering. The major theme is that **"even those who are fully aware of Christ' return are not prepared when He comes."** Jesus separated them as **"five being wise, and five being foolish."** This is not the first time in Matthew's gospel Jesus used the words "wise and foolish." He also used it in Matthew 7:24-27 when He used another word picture to teach about two different kinds of people in the world, some wise and some foolish. I believe the insight of that message has a link to the parable of the Ten Virgins.

In Matthew 7, Jesus said the wise man is the one who hears these sayings of mine and **does what he has been taught to do**. The foolish man is the one who hears but he **does not do what he**

has been taught to do. I believe this simple and basic truth helps us understand the message of the Ten Virgins. Let me make the connection.

First of all, what I find interesting about this parable is that the picture Jesus painted involved ten people. Unmistakably, the ten virgins are believers. It is a picture of the church in the end times, and the bridegroom is our Lord and Savior Jesus Christ.

They were all in one place doing the same thing; they "went forth to meet the bridegroom" (Kind of like going to church on Sunday morning). All ten virgins knew about the coming of the bridegroom but not all were prepared. Five were caught at an unexpected time with no oil in their lamps which symbolized not being prepared for His return. Remember, this is the continued theme of the three parables, the unexpected return. This is the difference between the wise and the foolish of Matthew 7. Could it be that they did not have oil because they simply did not do the things Jesus said to do? It is not just hearing the teachings of Christ but living out by faith what you have heard and been taught by Him.

THE MISSING INGREDIENT...FAITH

This is a perfect picture of what I see from a pastor's perspective. We have a whole generation that has heard the gospel but so precious few who actually do the things the Bible teaches us to do. The missing ingredient, faith! The oil that the five foolish did not have can only make reference to one thing and that is faith. It takes faith to continue on and persevere as we await for the return of the Lord. It is not about knowing that He is coming back because all ten knew of His return.

This is a composite of the day in which we live. Many people have heard the message of the return of Christ but they do not have any oil in their lamp, which means they do not have a genuine faith in God. A genuine faith in God motivates you to persevere and continue to do the work of God in the midst of great adversity. I assure you, there will be great adversity when one sets his heart to do the work of God. These five virgins knew a few facts about this Christian life or perhaps at one time they had an experience with God, but at the time of His return they have no oil, or no genuine faith.

You may be reading this book and say, "I already know all these things." The question is not do you know them, but do you have oil in your lamp? Are you doing what God told you to do as a true disciple of Christ? The sobering message of this parable is when the Lord returns there will be many who know all these things that Jesus did and said but will not be prepared for the Rapture and will be left behind.

Real and genuine faith is defined in Hebrews chapter eleven. In that chapter the writer highlights some of the great Old Testament hero's of faith. As he briefly summarizes the life of these men and women he testifies of what they did because of their faith, such as, "By faith Abel offered a more excellent sacrifice...". The word sacrifice tells us what his faith caused him to do. "By faith Noah...prepared an ark" Noah's faith was reflective in what he did, he built an ark. "By faith Abraham when he was called to go out...obeyed" Abraham's faith caused him to obey God and follow Him even when he didn't know where he was going. Real and genuine faith moves the believer to action which is reflective in the way he lives his life.

In verse eight in the parable there is an interesting message for our younger generation, *"And the foolish said to the wise, 'Give us some of your oil, for our lamps are going out"*. I say this is to our younger generation for this reason. Many today have raised their children in the church. They have been to Children's Church, Sunday School, Vacation Bible School and many other ministries the local church has provided for decades. Sadly, many of them have not learned what their parents have learned and that is how to live and walk by faith. Sometimes I believe it is because we as parents have not released them to the faith. Our compassion gets in the way as we continually bail them out of their troubles.

Everyone must learn to walk the walk of faith which means eventually you have to come to know the God of your parents and do the things they have done. You must learn to persevere in faith and serve Him in an uncompromising way. Too many in this generation are living on the faith of their parents or someone else that is close to them and not developing their own walk of faith with God.

There are several more significant points in this parable that I can't overlook. I will deal with them in the order in which Jesus gave them.

THE MIDNIGHT CRY

Notice when the bridegroom came, *"And at midnight a cry was heard: 'Behold, the bridegroom is coming; go out to meet him!"* We have another word picture, a metaphor. The key word is "midnight." Several thoughts come to mind when I think of midnight. First of all, it is dark. Leading up to the return of Christ the world will become a dark place. I don't mean as in light of day or darkness that comes with the going down of the sun. The world is becoming a dark place filled with the evil works of men as man continues to reject the light of the gospel.

> The world is becoming a dark place filled with the evil works of men as man continues to reject the light of the gospel.

When it is dark we lose our vision; we cannot see where we are going. This is our present world, leaders all around the world including the U.S. have no light. They do not know where they are going as they try to lead the people and their countries. The world is broke but no one knows how to fix what has been broken because there is no light. They simply cannot see.

Another thought that comes to mind when I think of midnight is, it is the end of one day and the beginning of another. This is a perfect picture of what will happen when the Lord returns. One day, a very long day, six thousand years of the history of man since Adam will come to an abrupt end. That will lead to the beginning of another day. For the believer that will go up in the Rapture, it will be the greatest day of our lives. Mortality will be changed to immortality as we leave this present world of darkness to face the greatest light the mind could ever imagine, the light of the presence of Almighty God.

For those who will be left behind, it also means the beginning of another day. It will be the first day of the greatest darkness the world has ever known as the clock begins to tick for the seven year Great Tribulation Period that Jesus spoke about Matthew 24:21 (KJV), " For then shall be great tribulation, such as was not since the beginning of the world to this time, no, nor ever shall be".

LIVE BY YOUR OWN FAITH NOT OURS...

Matthew 25:8 (KJV), " And the foolish said unto the wise, Give us of your oil; for our lamps are gone out". Listen carefully. Those who have refused to live and walk by their own faith in God will eventually be cut off by the faithful. "But the wise answered, saying, Not so, lest there be not enough for us and you..." There will come a point leading up to the return of the Lord that hardship will become so great that the only ones that will be able to survive what is happening on the earth are those who know how to live and walk by faith.

We live in an age where the poor and needy have learned that the local church and God's faithful people are benevolent. Because of their benevolent heart, they have helped the needy with every need imaginable for centuries. Sadly, the overwhelming majority of them have become dependent on the faith of other people. Having been given ample opportunity to change their lives and become responsible people, they have refused, and have become very content to live on someone else's faith.

As the day of the Lord draws near, the resources of the church are becoming strained to the point that the church will no longer be able to do things they have done in the past. **And this will be according to the will of God!** We live in the **"Entitlement Generation"**. Almost daily people come to the church looking for financial assistance. Many have the attitude that the church and the government exist to enable them to live their irresponsible lives. This day is quickly coming to an end. The message of the faithful five virgins is quickly becoming the message of the faithful in our day (Matthew 24:9) *"...go rather to them that sell and buy for yourselves."* They were saying we cannot do this for you anymore. This is a faith issue, and you must live by your own faith, not ours!

> **M**any have the attitude that the church and the government exist to enable them to live their irresponsible lives. This day is quickly coming to an end.

This is beginning to happen right now all across the world. The economic crisis has had a profound effect on the church in the U.S. One way this has impacted the church is in the mission budget of many churches. For more than half a century the church in the U.S. has funded churches in second and third world countries.

Budget cuts in American churches have caused many to stop their support to these foreign churches. A Bishop from a fellowship in India with over 2,000 churches recently told me he lost more than 50% of his financial support from the U.S. over the past few years.

What does it mean? God is saying, **"It is time for these churches to begin to live on their own faith not the faith of the American people"**.

The parable goes on to reveal that the foolish went their way attempting to do things they should have done many years before. But it was too late! The bridegroom had come and gone and in verse 11-12 the scripture says, *"Afterward the other virgins came also, saying, Lord, Lord, open to us. But he answered and said, Assuredly, I say to you, I do not know you."* It is too late, the time of opportunity has expired and they have been left behind.

In Luke 18:1-8, Jesus gave us the parable we call **"The Persistent Widow."** In this parable He teaches the necessity of being persistent in prayer. At the close of the parable He says *"...when the Son of Man comes, will He really find faith on the earth?"* Luke 18:8. The parable of the persistent widow and the parable of the ten virgins teach us that if we want to take part in the Rapture of the church we must be living and walking in a genuine faith in God or we will be left behind. Perhaps this is why Paul urged his followers to *"Examine yourself to know if you are in the faith or not"* (2 Corinthians 13:5).

Faith & Adversity

Today many are faced with great adversity. It is difficult for a pastor to watch the people he loves go through times of adversity and distress. And for some reason there seems to be more of it today than in days gone by. However, there is one thing I have observed with people in such times, they pray more, get closer to God and their faith increases. Perhaps the reason the Lord has to allow some adversity in our lives is because He knows that without it, we would not be living in a real and genuine faith when the trumpet sounds.

The adversity that we detest may be the very thing that prepares us for that which is before us. *"When the Son of man comes will He find faith?"*

THIRD PARABLE: THE PARABLE OF THE TALENTS

I marvel at the continued wisdom of our Lord as He prepares us for His return. I pray His wisdom be upon us all as we prepare for that great day when we meet Him face to face.

After the teaching about the Ten Virgins, I would have thought Jesus would have left the subject of preparedness. But not our Lord! There is another enlightening truth He wants to bring to our attention before He brings the subject to a close. We call it the "Parable of the Talents."

> [14] *"For the kingdom of heaven is like a man traveling to a far country, who called his own servants and delivered his goods to them. [15] And to one he gave five talents, to another two, and to another one, to each according to his own ability; and immediately he went on a journey. [16] Then he who had received the five talents went and traded with them, and made another five talents. [17] And likewise he who had received two gained two more also. [18] But he who had received one went and dug in the ground, and hid his lord's money. [19] After a long time the lord of those servants came and settled accounts with them.*

²⁰"So he who had received five talents came and brought five other talents, saying, 'Lord, you delivered to me five talents; look, I have gained five more talents besides them.' ²¹ His lord said to him, 'Well done, good and faithful servant; you were faithful over a few things, I will make you ruler over many things. Enter into the joy of your lord.' ²² He also who had received two talents came and said, 'Lord, you delivered to me two talents; look, I have gained two more talents besides them.' ²³ His lord said to him, 'Well done, good and faithful servant; you have been faithful over a few things, I will make you ruler over many things. Enter into the joy of your lord.'

²⁴"Then he who had received the one talent came and said, 'Lord, I knew you to be a hard man, reaping where you have not sown, and gathering where you have not scattered seed. ²⁵ And I was afraid, and went and hid your talent in the ground. Look, there you have what is yours.'

²⁶ "But his lord answered and said to him, 'You wicked and lazy servant, you knew that I reap where I have not sown, and gather where I have not scattered seed. ²⁷ So you ought to have deposited my money with the bankers, and at my coming I would have received back my own with interest. ²⁸ Therefore take the talent from him, and give it to him who has ten talents.

²⁹ 'For to everyone who has, more will be given, and he will have abundance; but from him who does not have, even what he has will be taken away. ³⁰ And cast the unprofitable servant into the outer darkness. There will be weeping and gnashing of teeth.'

Matthew 25:14-30

Jesus sets the stage with these words, *"For the kingdom of heaven is like a man traveling to a far country, who called his own servants and delivered his goods to them."* What a word picture the Lord created in such few words about the age of the church!

After the Lord was resurrected from the dead (Acts 1:1-11), He said His last words to His disciples, then He ascended into heaven where He has been for the last 2,000 years. In this parable Jesus is the man traveling to a far country, which began with His ascension. The servants He called and to whom He delivered His goods are His disciples, the modern day church, if you are a Christian that means you. His goods are the many gifts and talents He has given to average ordinary men and women to do the work of the ministry in the age of the church.

Many years later the Apostle Paul would give us insight into this parable when he wrote to the church at Ephesus in Ephesians 4:7-11. Not wanting to give an exposition on this passage, I will summarize it in just a few words. Jesus gave us, the church, His goods, which represent the many and varied gifts of God that reside in each of us enabling us to do the work of the ministry which began 2,000 years ago. There are other places in Paul's writings where he makes mention of the gifts of God that have been given to the believer, Romans chapter 12 and First Corinthians chapter 12.

> His goods are the many gifts and talents He has given to average ordinary men and women to do the work of the ministry in the age of the church.

The message of the parable is simple; we will give an account to God for what we have done with what He has given to us. God has bestowed upon all men and women gifts or talents as described in the parable, therefore, it is our responsibility in life to take that which has been given to us, cultivate it, nurture it to its full potential and invest it as we await the Lord's return.

In Proverbs 18:16 the wise man Solomon said, "A man's gift makes room for him, And brings him before great men". Have you discovered your God-given Gifts? The parable teaches several important truths about life that we should all be familiar with.

- All good gifts come from God.
- The gift of God in you is the key to your success in life.
- Although we all have equal opportunity to know God, we have not all been given the same number of Gifts or talents.
- When He comes back He wants to see what you have done with what you have been given.
- He will reward us according to how we have invested the gift of God within us.
- Some will suffer terrible loss because they did not use what God gave to them.

You may ask, "Why would this be so important in the light of His return?" For this reason, "God is depending on you and me to take the message of the Gospel of the Kingdom to the ends of the earth, and He needs your gift (or talent) to make this happen." The assignment to evangelize the world has been given to His church (Matthew 28:19-20) and the only way this can happen is if each of us takes what has been given, devotes it to Christ and follows the path He has before us.

In Matthew 24:14 Jesus said, "And this gospel of the kingdom will be preached in all the world as a witness to all the nations, and then the end will come." This is our God-given responsibility to the world, and it is at the very heart of the parable of the talents.

Remember the "When" question, "When will Jesus come back?" As we have learned no one knows the exact time of His return. However, Jesus said in the preceding verse that He would come back after we finished what He has given us to do, and that is, to evangelize the world. Know this—the investment of your talent is necessary for this to happen.

This parable closes with a strong condemnation upon one of the servants because he was so overwhelmed with fear that he hid his talent instead of using it and investing it for a return. The bottom line is, if we do not invest and use what has been freely given to us by God, the end result will be that some people will never hear the gospel and come to know Christ as their savior. We as Christians know that if they do not hear and respond to the gospel, they will spend eternity in a devil's hell. There can be no other explanation for the harsh condemning judgment to the one who hid his talent. Jesus' final words in Matthew 25:30 *"...cast the unprofitable servant into outer darkness. There will be weeping and gnashing of teeth."*

All this has been written to bring to our awareness the unexpected return of our Lord. I hold tightly to the words of the Apostle Paul in I Thessalonians 5:4-6, *"But you brethren, are not in darkness, so that this Day should overtake you as a thief. You are all sons of light and sons of day. We are not of the night, nor of darkness. Therefore let us not sleep; as others do, but let us watch and be sober"* and in verse 9 he said, *" For God did not appoint us to wrath, but to obtain salvation through our Lord Jesus Christ"*.

AMERICA AND BIBLE PROPHECY

CHAPTER 7

The most common question I am asked when teaching on the subject of Bible Prophecy is, "Can America be found in Bible Prophecy"? The answer is yes, but not in the way we would hope. There is only one place in Eschatological studies where direct reference is made to the western hemisphere:

> *"Sheba, Dedan, the merchants of Tarshish, and all their young lions will say to you, Have you come to take plunder? Have you gathered your army to take booty, to carry away silver and gold, to take away livestock and goods, to take great plunder?"*
>
> Ezekiel 38:13

Many scholars believe this passage of scripture is addressed to western nations including Great Britain, Europe and the United States of America. I touched on this in chapter two in the Gog and Magog War. The context in which it is written speaks volumes to us about America and other western nations.

The scene is the Gog and Magog War, a time in the near future when Russia, Iran and Arab nations come across the deserts of the Middle East committed to the destruction of Israel. As these countries align themselves and prepare for an invasion of Israel, the West responds with a passive, gutless attitude about what is taking place. I have already addressed the possible reasons why this attitude might exist in chapter two.

WHY NOT MORE ABOUT AMERICA?

The fact that little is said about America in Bible prophecy has baffled Bible students for more than half a century. Why so little would be said about the greatest nation that ever existed is incomprehensible to many. There are a few possible reasons why I believe this to be so.

First of all, America is not the only significant nation in our present world about which the Bible is silent. There is Canada, the continent of South America and the many nations found on that continent. We also have Australia, New Zealand, Middle and Southern African nations, South Korea, and many great developing nations in Asia. **We must remember the Bible is about the Middle East, and particularly the land of Israel and the Jewish people.** Also, nations that are significant in modern times did not exist in the era of Biblical writings.

Another question that surfaces now is, "Why would the Iraq war be mentioned ,but WW I and WW II not be mentioned in Bible Prophecy?" The answer would be the same; neither of those wars specifically involved the Middle East. These wars were significant to the unfolding of the End Times, but they were not about the Middle East.

As we have seen in previous chapters, the only nations of significance in the prophetic writings about the End Times are ancient Persia, which is Iran, Rosh, Meshech and Tubal. They represent the geographical regions of the former Soviet Union, North African countries, Israel and other bordering nations of Israel. In Revelation chapter 16 there is also mention of the Kings of the East which represents China and other Asian nations but it does not mention them specifically.

Another possibility is that the superpowers of our time cease to exist as the End Times unfold. Some will argue that scenario can't be possible. However, if you would have said to first century Rome that eventually it would cease to exist as a world power, the Romans would have thought you were mad and you might have been executed. Today, Rome is a tourist attraction and only known for her history, not for her present status on the world scene.

What about China?

Some believe China could have a role in the Gog and Magog war in Ezekiel 38 and 39. In Revelation 16:12 the prophetic word mentions the *"Kings from the East..."*, which I believe is primarily China, India and Indonesia. In the prophecy the Kings of the East are pictured crossing the Euphrates to war against Mystery Babylon during the War of Armageddon.

Today, the free world has great fear of communist China. China presents herself as economically strong, but China has a developing weakness that poses a great threat to her existence. China is vulnerable to a humanitarian health crisis that could develop into a pandemic equal to that of the black plague of the 1400's.

China has a population of over one billion people but refuses to develop the infrastructure to maintain and manage such a large population. A pandemic could wipe out two-thirds of that nation's population in just a few weeks time. This nation invites such a catastrophe because a large part of her population lives in or near some of the most massive landfills in the world.

> China has oppressed the poor for centuries; and no nation in history that has oppressed the poor has continued to prosper.

Although China appears to be economically strong, her development as a nation is so far behind her population it is hard to believe they can continue to exist much longer. Something of a catastrophic nature could happen in her near future that will be according to Biblical proportions. She could cease to exist as a power overnight and become a land of sickness and death as prophesied in the book of Revelation. Also, China has oppressed the poor for centuries; and no nation in history that has oppressed the poor has continued to prosper. Eventually, China will fail economically just as other nations of the world.

AMERICA THE BEAUTIFUL

In the first draft of this book I deliberately chose not to say much about America. I made a few brief statements about the U.S. but purposely did not give a great deal of detail. What I have written in this chapter and chapter 8 came from a little prodding by those who contributed to editing the final draft. More than one editor and a trusted friend requested I give more thought to what I see for the future of the U.S. according to Scripture. The reason I initially wanted to avoid this subject is revealed in the following pages. What I have written is difficult, at least for me because of the love I have for this great land and people.

The following pages will be challenging for many. I realize I risk alienating some because of what I am about to say, but if I were silent, I would violate my conscience and have to answer to God. When I first began writing this book, I committed to the Lord that I would stay true to my conscience, regardless of the possible misunderstanding by a few.

Please note: what you are about to read is based on moral convictions born out of a revelation of the God of the Bible. I have no political agenda, and although I belonged to a particular political party for most of my adult life, I recently decided to separate myself from that party. My convictions have been formed by the moral law revealed in the Bible and I could really care less about Democrat, Republican, Independent or Tea Party. I am first and foremost a Christian. Thirty–seven years ago God called me to preach the message of Christ to my generation and this book is part of the fulfilling of that call upon my life. It is Christ I choose to please and no one else.

America, the greatest nation in the history of man is in great trouble. We have morphed into an idolatrous people who have forsaken our covenant with God. Many live as though God doesn't exist. Have you ever loved something so much that it hurts? I love America; I love the people of America. I love the multifaceted cultures that make up this great country. We are truly a unique and colorful people. **We are America the beautiful.** My love for our country and the world has given me a great passion to do all I can to preach the message of Christ with the hope that some, as the people of Nineveh did in the book of Jonah, will hear, believe and call upon the Lord.

THE IMMUTABILITY OF GOD

History reveals the immutable character and person of the God of the Bible. There are three irrefutable truths that interpret life for me personally and us as a nation. This means I understand life based upon these three truths: **1. History**, as revealed in God's word the Bible. **2. Eschatological studies in the subject of prophecy,** which is a revelation of what God has said will happen leading up to the return of Christ. **3. Moral Judgment,** as revealed in the Bible. What I have written about America is based upon these three immutable truths. All truth is immutable, for truth and immutability are both attributes of God. Immutability means unchanging. God is immutable; He never changes. The writer of Hebrews said, He changes not (Hebrews 6:17). The same is said of truth. Truth never changes because God and truth are one and the same. Scripture says that Jesus is the same yesterday, today and forever. He never changes. He is the way, the truth and the life.

Understanding what God expects of people is very clearly revealed in the written Word of God, *"Now all these things happened to them as examples, and they were written for our admonition, upon whom the ends of the ages have come"* (I Corinthians 10:11). The study of the immutability of God reveals to us what He is doing presently and what He will do in the future as it pertains to his immutable truth. Therefore, history and the immutability of God reveal the future of America and all nations and people of the world, as it pertains to the moral standard revealed in the historical inspired writings of scripture.

THE WEDDING DINNER

In the study of scripture I am continually amazed at the many similarities between America and Israel. In the Old Testament Israel became the covenant people of God with a God-given mission to establish His covenant in all the earth (Deuteronomy 8:18). America came to rise in the 20th century as the largest Christian nation ever to exist, and like Israel, was given a mission to take the message of Christ to the nations of the world. There are many strong similarities between America and Israel of the Old Testament writings. One illustration of this is in the parable of the "Wedding Dinner".

In Matthew 22:1-14, Jesus used a parable to convey a profound message to His disciples in simple story form. This parable is called **"The Wedding Dinner"** and in it Jesus, the master teacher, shows the invitation given by God the Father to the Nation of Israel to join Him in what scripture calls, **"The Marriage Supper of the Lamb".** He began with these words, *"The kingdom of heaven is like a certain king who arranged a marriage for his son".*

In the parable Jesus told of **two distinct invitations** given to the Jewish people to join the **"Wedding Dinner".** *"...And sent out his servants to call those who were invited to the wedding; and they were not willing to come".* **The First invitation** speaks of Old Testament times revealed by the prophets. Yet the Nation of Israel and its people would not come. They refused to hear the message and stoned the prophets as Old Testament history shows.

The Second invitation was issued by other messengers like John the Baptist, Jesus, and the Apostles who followed Christ as the Church was being birthed. *"...Again, he sent out other servants, saying, Tell those who are invited, See, I have prepared my dinner; my oxen and fatted cattle are killed, and all things are ready. Come to the wedding. But they made light of it and went their own ways...seized his servants, treated them spitefully and killed them".* This refers to the persecution of Christians by the Jews which led to the crucifixion of Jesus and the martyrdom of many in the first century church.

Jesus continued the parable, *"...But when the king heard about it, he was furious. And he sent out his armies, destroyed these murderers, and burned up their city".* This points to the destruction of the city of Jerusalem and the burning of the temple in 70 A.D.

by the Romans. He continued, "...*Then he said to his servants, the wedding is ready, but those who were invited were not worthy*". Again He is speaking of the Jews who were not worthy of the "Wedding Dinner" because they rejected the Messiah. Jesus went on to say, "...*Therefore go into the highways, and as many as you find, invite to the wedding*". And this has been the ministry of the Church for the past 2,000 years, inviting as many as are willing to come, both Jew and Gentile. We call it the Great Commission; the invitation is to all who are willing, and that includes You the reader.

The Marriage Supper he is referring to here will take place in heaven after the Rapture of the Church with the saints of God and the heavenly host. It will be at the same time the people on the earth will be experiencing the horrible things that will happen during the Great Tribulation Period. What a paradox! The Wedding Dinner is mentioned in Revelation 19:7-10, right before the Second Coming of Christ.

THE REJECTION OF JESUS...

The Jews, God's chosen people made a choice; their choice was to reject Jesus Christ the Son of God. The rejection of Christ caused great and grievous consequences to the Jewish people for nearly 2,000 years. The city of Jerusalem was destroyed and the temple burned with fire by the Romans. The Jews were scattered all over the world from 70 A.D. until 1948. Today they are the most persecuted and hated people on the face of the earth, all because they rejected Jesus Christ, the Son of God.

The world has yet to understand the depth of the despicable, heinous sin of rejecting Jesus Christ, God's only begotten Son. To encounter Him and reject Him is both a sin and a crime. The writer of Hebrews said in reference to those who have encountered the Christ and yet reject Him, "...*seeing they crucify to themselves the*

Son of God afresh, and put Him to an open shame" (Hebrews 6:6).

The sacrificial giving of God's Son is incomprehensible for most. I have been blessed with two children I absolutely adore. I have given up my rights to many things in this life for the cause of Christ: houses, lands, relationships with family and friends. For the cause of Christ my wife Dianna and I have forfeited opportunities for high paying jobs and potentially lucrative business opportunities. We have done this many times in 31 years of marriage, without regret. I can't think of one thing we wouldn't give up for the sake of the Gospel. But, my children…I don't think so…!

You can have my car; you can have my house; you can have my money…But my children? My girls are the apple of my eye; don't even think about it…! My life yes, their lives…No! You would agree when it comes to your children. But, in Romans 8:32 Scripture says, *"He who did not spare His own Son, but delivered Him up for us all…"*

God spared nothing to give us salvation. When He gave us Jesus there was nothing left to give. Because this is God's loving, sacrificial gift to the world, and when the gift is rejected, it becomes the single greatest sin and crime a human being can commit in this life. It is a sin worthy of death and damnation. There is really only one sin that will eternally damn a person's soul to a devil's hell, and that sin is the rejection of Jesus Christ. To reject Jesus once He has been offered to you, will make you just as guilty as the murderous crowd that shouted, "Crucify Him, Crucify Him", to Pontius Pilate.

GOD BLESS AMERICA...?

Today, American's are faced with a sobering question. Are we guilty of the same sin Israel committed in the first century? Israel was God's covenant people as portrayed in Old Testament history. In modern times the U.S. represents the largest people group that has embraced Christianity since the birth of Christ. But in the likeness of Israel we have broken our covenant with God and today have become the Prodigal of the New Covenant.

As America continues to reject Christ we are confronted with this sobering question, have we crucified afresh the Son of God and put Him to an open shame? If we are, history reveals our destiny. If God would not turn his head and excuse His chosen people, the Jews 2,000 years ago, why should we think He would look the other way while America commits the same crime the Jews did in history?

Because of the immutability of God, His judgment on Israel in the first century set forth an example to every nation and people thereafter. Every nation that has persecuted Christianity during the past 2,000 years eventually ceased to exist as a significant power and influence in world history. Some may argue, "but this is the dispensation of Grace" and that is true. However, this judgment on the Jews was executed during the dispensation of grace, which followed Jesus' death on the cross!

God has been removed from our culture in the U.S. The Ten Commandments have been removed from public facilities in all 50 states: Courtrooms, Capital Buildings, Class rooms, and more. Prayer has been banned in our schools and Biblical teaching is nowhere to be found in curriculum. You will find books on witchcraft in the libraries of our public schools but it is rare to find a Bible. A teacher can have her class read Harry Potter (witchcraft) for an assignment, but if she had a Bible on her desk in plain sight of her students, she could lose her job.

Our nation was recently shaken by the horrible shooting in

Newtown, Connecticut. Days following the event everyone was frantically trying to analyze what went wrong with this 20 year old young man who shot and killed 26 people, including 20 grade school children. Because of the age of the children and the cold blooded way in which they were killed, I would estimate it to be the most horrid atrocity in U.S. history since the Civil War.

Shortly after the shooting, the Church began to cry out, "Put God back in the classroom". Our voices were quickly silenced by the liberal agenda of gun control. They are blind guides leading the blind! Morality...Morality...is the problem, a lack of it! Remove God and you throw morality to the wind. When we say put God back in the classroom, we are saying put morality back in the classroom. And, moral excellence cannot be sustained if it does not originate with God and the Bible.

The Law of Accountability

There are several spiritual laws that are working against America today. One is the Law of Accountability. Scripture says *"...to whom much is given, from him much will be required;"* (Luke 12:48). The American people have been given more opportunities to know Christ than any other people on the planet. You can hardly turn a street corner without passing another church. Bibles are everywhere, by the tens of millions. Radio, television, newspapers, magazines and on and on. This nation has been saturated with the message of the saving grace of Jesus Christ. Therefore, America will be held to a higher level of accountability than other nations that have barely heard the message.

In Matthew 11:20-24 Jesus warned the cities of Chorazin, Bethsaida and Capernaum. He told them that because of the miraculous things that were done by Him in those cities, it would be more tolerable for Sodom, Tyre and Sidon in the day of judgment than it would be for them. We know according to Old Testament history that God destroyed those cities because of their sinfulness. Jesus was saying to those cities in the first century, you will be held accountable for what you have heard and seen. God holds everyone accountable for what they have heard and seen in their lifetime, *"to whom much is given, from him much will be required;"*.

THE LAW OF RECIPROCITY

Another spiritual law that is working against America is the Law of Reciprocity. In Galatians 6, Paul said to the Church, *"Do not be deceived, God is not mocked; for whatever a man sows, that he will also reap"* (Galatians 6:7). It is also called the Law of Sowing and Reaping.

God set these laws in motion to be a blessing to man, and when the moral standard of God is honored; they have the potential to usher in the blessings of the Kingdom of God in such a way that they can change a world. However, when they are not honored by adherence to the moral revelation of the Word of God, they will work against you as an individual, or as a nation.

JUDGMENT OF THE NATIONS

In the Olivet Discourse (Matthew 25:31-46), Jesus said there would be a "Judgment of the Nations". Chronologically, Jesus Himself said it will be, *"When the Son of Man comes in His glory, and the holy angels with Him, then He will sit on the throne of His glory"*. This will take place after the War of Armageddon when Jesus sits on His throne in Jerusalem to rule the world in the Millennial Reign. The Nations of the world will be judged and held accountable to God for what they have done with Jesus and the authority that was entrusted to them by God.

Every politician needs to realize that they will answer to God for how they have managed the affairs of the nations of the world. *"Let every soul be subject to the governing authorities. For there is no authority except from God, and the authorities that exist are **appointed by God**"*, Romans 13:1. Notice the scripture says, **"Appointed by God";** it does not say **"Approved by God". Appointing and Approving are two different things. God's appointing is based upon their potential, not upon His foreknowledge of what they may or may not do in the future. If those who are in politics understood their God-given responsibility and the accountability that will follow, fewer would aspire to political office.**

There is a continual unfolding of judgment in America today because of the rejection of Jesus Christ. At one time America boasted itself to be a Christian Nation, and in past history this may have been true, but today no such claim can be made. Over 80 percent of American people profess Christianity. Yet 50 percent or more cast their vote for politicians that support the murder of innocent unborn babies.

When this horrid event took place in Connecticut, (December 14, 2012) we all mourned for days and weeks thereafter. Some said, "Life will never be the same". I applaud all for their heartfelt sympathy for the loss incurred by these families. However, many of us grieve perpetually for the more than 54 million unborn babies that have been slaughtered in the name of "Pro Choice". Thankfully, today they are all in heaven with our loving heavenly Father.

Our government and the medical profession have told this generation that the life inside a pregnant woman isn't really a baby until it is born. I ask the simple question, "What if you are wrong...? What if...?" And according to the Bible you are wrong! God said to the Prophet Jeremiah, *"Before I formed you in the womb I*

knew you; Before you were born I sanctified you; I ordained you a prophet to the nations" (Jeremiah 1:5). God recognized the person and the purpose for Jeremiah's existence before he was ever born. Should we not do the same?

In Titus 1:16 , Paul said, *"...in works they deny Him"*. Once again we are confronted with a sobering question: "Is it possible that the Pro Choice agenda has made us guilty of denying Christ the Savior of the world"? **Is America and other nations of the world guilty before God? Have we all committed the heinous crime of crucifying the Son of God afresh and putting Him to public shame?**

WILL AMERICA PROSPER AGAIN?

Politicians campaign and make promises to rebuild America's struggling economy. What arrogance...! Do they not know...? Do they not understand...? The economical woes of America and the world are due to the continual rejection of the Son of God. The spiritual laws I just mentioned are working against us. Because of them, there is no financial genius on earth that can reverse this downward economic crisis. **You cannot print or borrow enough money to cover the sin of rejecting Jesus Christ the Son of God!**

The Word of God reveals a truth that most will not acknowledge. That truth is, "God will not cry out forever"! The patience of God and the mercy of God will eventually be withdrawn from a people who continually refuse to be moved by it. This is what happened to the Jews in the first century as revealed in the parable of, "The Wedding Dinner". After hundreds of years of God's patience and mercy He drew a line and said, "There will be no more", and judgment came upon them as Rome invaded Jerusalem and the Jewish people lost their identity for nearly 2,000 years.

It is my sincere opinion that America, this land that I love, has reached this place with God. I say that with much pain and grief. I say that with fear and trembling, knowing full well what it means for us, our children and grandchildren. America has abused the mercy, patience and grace of God. This is why I am writing this book. This is why the message must go forth calling all that will hear to the cross of Christ. Jesus said the world would once

> Have you ever loved something so much that it hurts? I love America; I love the people of America. I love the multifaceted cultures that make up this great country. We are truly a unique and colorful people. We are America the beautiful.

again become, "...*As it was in the days of Noah*". God numbered the days of their final existence and when that time expired, they ceased to exist as God judged them for their evil deeds.

THE EARTH IS THE LORD'S

In Deuteronomy 8:18 God said: *"And you shall remember the Lord your God, for it is He who gives you power to get wealth..."*

In Psalm 24:1 (KJV) the Psalmist said, *"The earth is the Lord's, and the fullness thereof; the world and they that dwell therein"*

Psalm 50:10 (KJV) the Lord said, *"For every beast of the forest is mine, and the cattle on a thousand hills"*

Haggai 2:8 (KJV) God said, *"The silver is mine, and the gold is mine, saith the Lord of hosts."*

These Scriptures clearly declare that the wealth of the earth belongs to God. If a nation or an individual expects to prosper and be blessed, he will need to be in the good graces of the one who holds the wealth. Any people who have crucified afresh the

Son of God cannot expect to be in good favor with the God of all creation.

The Point Of No Return

I believe America has reached the point of no return. We have insulted the spirit of grace as mentioned in the book of Hebrews chapter ten.

> *26For if we sin willfully after we have received the knowledge of the truth, there no longer remains a sacrifice for sins, 27 but a certain fearful expectation of judgment, and fiery indignation which will devour the adversaries. 28 Anyone who has rejected Moses' law dies without mercy on the testimony of two or three witnesses. 29 Of how much worse punishment, do you suppose, will he be thought worthy who has trampled the Son of God underfoot, counted the blood of the covenant by which he was sanctified a common thing, and insulted the Spirit of grace? 30 For we know Him who said, "Vengeance is Mine, I will repay," says the Lord. And again, "The Lord will judge His people." 31 It is a fearful thing to fall into the hands of the living God.*
>
> Hebrews 10:26-31

These scriptures are difficult, but we must remember, the Bible is not like a smorgasbord in a restaurant where you take what you want and leave the rest. These things were written for this generation just as much as John 3:16 and all other passages we adore in His blessed book.

For the reasons I have already stated I believe we have trampled the Son of God underfoot, counted the blood of the covenant a common thing and insulted the Spirit of grace just as Scripture warned us not to do. We are guilty! And because we are guilty, we continue to move farther away from His grace and have reached **a point of no return.**

The Land of Paradoxes

America is filled with paradoxes. There is good, and there is the evil. The problem is, in my life time I have seen evil increase at an exponential rate. The good has become despised and rejected just as Jesus and His disciples were in their day. And evil is applauded, legalized and encouraged by many.

There are good God-loving people in America. I believe some of the most moral and honorable people in the world can be found inside the borders of this great land. But that which has made us great is also that which has become a festering disease, "Democracy"! In government democracy is the greatest thing on earth. And at the same time democracy can be a great evil because of its inherit weakness. **It will only be as good or as bad as are the core values of the people that make up the democracy.**

There was a time when democracy served us and made us great, but now it is the very thing that is destroying us from within. When the influence of the moral excellence found in the Bible was separated from education and government, lawmakers didn't realize they were dismantling America by their poor judgment. When this happened, the core values of American people changed. When our core values changed so did our great nation. It is what was in the heart of America that made it different and greater than other nations of the world. America is truly being destroyed from within, within the heart of a generation that doesn't know the God of our fathers.

Baby Jessica

America is a land of paradoxes. In October of 1987 an 18 month old toddler became known to the world as "Baby Jessica". Baby Jessica accidently fell 22 feet down an 8 inch well pipe. It took rescuers 59 hours to finally rescue her from what almost became her grave. The whole nation was mesmerized by this horrid event. News teams from across the nation were covering it minute by minute. It seemed that the only thing that mattered to anyone was the rescue of this little toddler who no one even known or heard of just hours before. People came from thousands of miles at their own expense to do what they could to help. After the event was over, almost $1,000,000.00 in donations had been sent to a special fund for "Baby Jessica" from people who didn't even know her.

Here is the paradox:

God, have mercy on us...

How can we explain that the same people who wanted to turn the world backwards on its axis to save Baby Jessica could be guilty of taking the lives of more than 54 million unborn innocent babies since Roe verses Wade in 1973? And we carry on seeking wealth and prosperity as though we were a moral civilized people who have done no wrong? History tells us that infanticide has been around for thousands of years and that no nation has ever survived this

> History tells us that infanticide has been around for thusands of years and that no nation has ever survived this atrocity. Every society that has exterminated their chldren eventually ceased to exist as a significant people.

atrocity. Every society that has exterminated their children eventually ceased to exist as a significant people.

Political leaders in Washington spout their master plan about how they will turn around the economy. They lack understanding about how real prosperity is achieved. Printing and borrowing money is not prosperity. You cannot borrow or print enough money to cover up the blood stained-hands from the millions of innocent unborn babies. The arrogance and spirit of Babel rests upon this land and it will bring us to ruin just as it did upon the people of the Tower of Babel in ancient history.

When Isaiah prophesied about the modern day destruction of Babylon (The Iraq War) he concluded his thoughts with some fearful words (Isaiah 13:6-13),

> *6 Wail, for the day of the Lord is at hand! It will come as destruction from the Almighty.*
> *7 Therefore all hands will be limp, Every man's heart will melt,*
> *8 And they will be afraid. Pangs and sorrows will take hold of them; They will be in pain as a woman in childbirth; They will be amazed at one another; Their faces will be like flames.*
> *9 Behold, the day of the Lord comes, Cruel, with both wrath and fierce anger, To lay the land desolate; And He will destroy its sinners from it.*
> *10 For the stars of heaven and their constellations Will not give their light; The sun will be darkened in its going forth, And the moon will not cause its light to shine.*
> *11 "I will punish the world for its evil, And the wicked for their iniquity; I will halt the arrogance of the proud, And will lay low the haughtiness of the terrible.*

Notice the words, *"Wail, for the day of the Lord is at hand"*. People are wailing, I hear them wail every time I turn on the news. The problem is only precious few are wailing for the right reasons. The majority I see wailing are those who make up the Entitlement Generation as they protest and wail for more free stuff. I would they were wailing for the unborn with the same passion they wail for free stuff.

The words, *"...the Lord is at hand"*, means that God will not be silent. Jesus is about to return! *"It will come as destruction from the Almighty."* That which is coming upon America and the world is from God Himself. No government can produce a bailout to res-cue us from this mess. One of the reasons the world will yield to a New World Order ruled by the Anti-Christ is because the nations of the world have become so weak economically and militarily they can no longer survive on their own. They will need a worldwide alliance to survive, *"...all hands will be limp, Every man's heart will melt, and they will be afraid"*.

"Pangs and sorrow will take hold of them; They will be in pain as a woman in child birth", A woman suffering the pain of birthing a child is helpless, she is totally dependent upon others even for the simple things, as simple as reaching for a glass of water.

The chronological order for this message is for the inhabitants of the earth after the close of the recent Iraq war. That means this is the message for this generation, the final message. *"...I will pun-ish the world for its evil, and the wicked for their iniquity; I will halt the arrogance of the proud, and will lay low the haughtiness of the terrible"*. But who will hear? Some will hear. There will always be some who will hear and call upon the name of the Lord. But it will not be the masses. It never has been.

I know this is a difficult word to digest. The reason it is so difficult is because the pulpit in America has abandoned the fundamental teachings of the Bible. Preachers have become the self help gurus of the modern world. Biblical Christianity is symbolized by a Cross, a Yoke and a Plow. Christianity in America today is symbolized by big money and million dollar homes. Because of the obsession with wealth, prosperity and personal achievement in the church, half of the message has never been heard by this present generation.

The Near Future for America

What I am going to say next will sound like I am prophesying the future of America but it is not a prophecy. My thoughts are based upon the spiritual laws I mentioned in the beginning of this chapter, the Law of Accountability and the Law of Reciprocity, and also what the Bible says will happen prophetically in the near future. I have already addressed some of these thoughts, but I would like to put them in perspective.

America will not recover economically. There are many reasons why this is so but the main reason is because our government has worshipped Mammon, or wealth. Greed is at the very heart of abortion. Abortion is not just about the "Freedom of choice" it is also about money and wealth. In I Timothy 6:10 Paul said "...the love of money is the root of all evil". And in II Timothy 3:2-4 he said *"Men will become lovers of themselves...lovers of pleasure more than lovers of God".*

It is the love of self and the love of money that causes a people to take the life of the unborn. Our government has decided it is more economically convenient to kill that baby before it is born, rather than risking the child becoming a burden of the state for a lifetime. It is about money and self! For this reason and this reason alone America will not recover economically.

The $16 trillion and counting deficit will never be paid off. They have no intentions of ever paying it off. The agenda is to devalue America economically to the level of other nations in the world. This will remove all opposition as we move toward to a one world economy and one world government. When the President said, "We need to spread the wealth", he wasn't talking about taking Bill Gates billions and sharing it with the poor. He was talking about his personal agenda of taking America's wealth and sharing it with other nations of the world which will devalue America to that of second and third world countries. This has to happen as the stage is being set for the rule of the Anti-Christ.

America will lose its military superpower status, simply because there will not be finances to sustain it. This too must happen before the rule of the Anti-Christ and a one world government takes place.

We will lose the right to preach the Bible in America. Taking a stand against homosexuality and other abominations will be considered hate crimes punishable by law.

If the return of Christ is delayed and the melt down continues eventually we will lose our freedom to worship corporately. Let me explain why I believe this can and will happen.

I present to you another similarity between that of the U.S. and ancient Israel. In 605 B.C. God brought judgment upon Israel because of their backsliding and idolatry and we are guilty of the same sins. The Israelites were taken into Babylonian captivity inside the walled city of ancient Babylon. They were made to be slaves, imprisoned by an oppressive pagan government. This time of history is recorded in the book of Daniel.

Because of their persistent rebellion against God, God took away all their freedoms. The freedom to live in their homeland

Israel was taken from them and also the freedom to worship their God. The only freedom they had in worship was what they could do as individuals, not in a corporate setting.

This is the principle: **"When the freedom entrusted to you has been misused and has become the instrument of rebellion against God, it will be taken from you"**. Every parent understands this discipline in raising children.

When my girls became teens, they began their struggle for freedom. This is normal. After several frustrating experiences of negotiating the boundaries, I finally said to them this is the plan. "You will determine how much freedom you will have". I established a boundary of what I thought was reasonable and I said to them, "If you stay within these boundaries and respect what you have been given after three months I will give you more. But if you violate the boundaries and fail to respect what we have agreed upon, I will take away that which has been given to you". We all agreed. I will write a book on family life one day and tell you the rest of the story.

God has entrusted America with a freedom unequal to any other nation in the world. We have ruled the world militarily and economically for nearly a century. But we have abused our freedom. God is our Father. He is a good parent and when we use the freedom He has given us for the wrong things, He will take it away from us.

> When the freedom entrusted to you has been misused and has become the instrument of rebellion against God, it will be taken from you.

The Abuse of Freedom

I will mention a few of the freedoms we have abused:

- **The Pro Choice agenda.** When we use freedom to take the life of the unborn we have become the God of our own universe.

  "There shall be no other God's before Me, says the Lord."

- **Same sex marriage.** When we use freedom to pervert our lifestyle and do that which is contrary to nature, we have become the God of a new creation that cannot coexist with the Biblical creation of man.

  "There shall be no other God's before Me, says the Lord."

- **Ordaining Homosexuals for Ministry.** When we use freedom to ordain what the Bible calls an abomination for ministry in the house of God, we have become the God of a double standard.

  "There shall be no other God's before Me, says the Lord."

- **Abuse of Authority.** When we use authority to encourage others to violate their moral convictions we have become the God of civilization.

  "There shall be no other God's before Me, says the Lord."

Freedom is not doing what you want to do; freedom is doing what you ought to do as revealed in the moral law of God. When man becomes a law unto himself, he has made himself the God of his own world. This is an abomination and God will not be silent. He will remove the freedoms from those who refuse to honor the moral law in His written word the Bible.

When the Anti-Christ rules the world, there will be a one world government, a one world economy and a one world religion. To accomplish such a global rule in all three areas tells me that freedom has ceased to exist as we know it today. The loss of freedom seems incomprehensible to our present world, yet this is exactly what Israel experienced in Babylonian captivity. Israel lost every freedom and every right God had given to them. They became slaves in a foreign land, where they did not belong.

Can what happened 2,600 years ago happen again? Not only can it happen but according to Biblical Prophecy, it will happen and lead to the Second Coming of Christ.

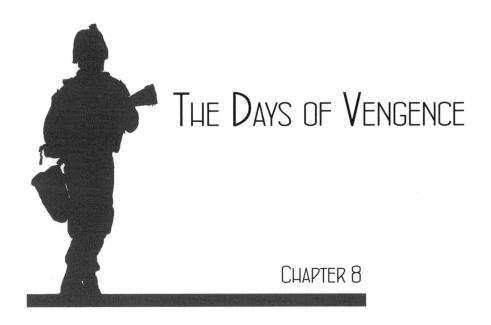

THE DAYS OF VENGENCE

CHAPTER 8

Jesus said in Luke 21:22, *"For these are the days of vengeance, that all things which are written may be fulfilled.."*

Jesus declared this present time as a day of vengeance. He then stated the reason why, *"...that all things which are written may be fulfilled"*.

For millenniums the righteous have suffered terrible injustices by the hate crimes of the ungodly. The statistics about the persecution of Christianity is startling. In the 20th century alone it is estimated that 35 million Christians died for their faith in Jesus Christ.

From 1920-1930 history reveals that 200,000 Russian Orthodox priests, monks and nuns were slaughtered because of their faith. Many were crucified by nailing them to the door of their churches. Some were stripped naked, doused with water and left to freeze in the sub-freezing temperatures. During the cultural revolution in China from 1960 – 1970's, 400,000 died for their faith in Christ.

In 1994, an estimated 500,000 were killed for their Christian faith in Rwanda. The lists of deaths over the past centuries are endless. Christians, like the Jews, are the most persecuted people on earth.

God will not remain silent! Jesus said, these are the days of vengeance. Every promise God has made to vindicate the righteous will be fulfilled.

THE PERSISTENT WIDOW

In Luke 18:1-8 Jesus told a parable that addresses this injustice and the promise to avenge the righteous. It is called the parable of "The Persistent Widow". In it the persistent widow petitions an unrighteous judge to avenge her of her adversaries. The scripture says that he would not for a while, but because of her persistence he eventually said, *"I will avenge her, lest by her continual coming she weary me"*.

Then the Lord said, *"Hear what the unjust judge said.* ***And shall God not avenge His own elect who cry out day and night to Him, though He bears long with them? I tell you that He will avenge them speedily."***

In the book of Genesis, chapter four, we have the story of two brothers, Cain and Abel. Cain killed his brother Abel because Cain's offering was not respected by God. After Cain murdered his brother God came to him and asked *"Where is Abel your brother?"* Cain said, *"I do not know, am I my brother's keeper?"* And God said, *"What have you done? The voice of your brother's blood cries out to me from the ground"*.

Consider, if the shedding of one man's blood cried out from the ground and captured the attention of God, how much more will God be moved by the cries of millions who continue to cry out day and night? There is a perpetual cry to God day and night from the millions who are waiting to be avenged of their adversaries. And Jesus said, *"...He will avenge them speedily".*

The day of vengeance has begun, God has assured the righteous that He will avenge them of their adversaries *"...Vengeance is Mine, I will repay, says the Lord"* (Hebrews 10:30).

I don't believe anyone can say with absolute certainty when the "Day of Vengeance" began. I do, however, believe it is already unfolding due to a few observations about things which have occurred over the past three decades.

The 1980's marked a significant time in the history of the Church and the secular world in the U.S. The Church reached its peak as the age of the mega church was born. In the late 70's and early 80's churches were exploding across America. Church planting was the order of the day. If a new church wasn't exploding on the scene, expansions and new building projects were everywhere.

At the same time the Church was experiencing unparalleled prosperity, so was the U.S. economy. The U.S. economy boomed. Industry grew exponentially and so did the U.S. war machine which drove the Soviet Union to economic collapse. Don't underestimate the connection of the prosperity of the Church and the prosperity of the economy. They are one and the same!

Then, in the late 80's something of prophetic significance began to sweep across the U.S. In I Peter 4:17, Peter said, *"For the time is come for judgment to begin at the house of God; if it begins with us first, what will be the end of those who do not obey the gospel".*

Judgment swept across the Church like wild fire in the late 80's.

Ministries began to fall as moral indiscretion dismantled the church world. The world stood in shock as many were humiliated and disillusioned by what was being revealed. But what was happening in the Church was only the prelude to what was yet to come. Peter said by the inspiration of the Holy Spirit, "...*if it begins with us first, what will be the end of those who do not obey the gospel of God?*" (I Peter 4:17).

I will list just a few of the world shaking events that began to unfold:

- The fall of Soviet Russia 1989
- The invasion of Kuwait in 1990
- The Gulf War of 1991
- The Oklahoma City bombing of 1995
- Scandal in the White House in 1998
- "9/11" - 2001
- Invasion of Afghanistan 2002
- Invasion of Iraq 2003
- Tsunami in Indonesia 2004
- Hurricane Katrina 2005
- Worldwide economical collapse in 2007 and 2008
- Hurricane Sandy 2012, etc., etc.

Judgment began in the house of God, but it didn't stop there. The "Day of Vengeance" began to unfold against all ungodliness. Jesus said in the Olivet Discourse that there would be a "Judgment of the Nations" when the Lord returned. What we are experiencing at present is not the judgment of the nations as prophesied by Jesus, for that will not happen until Christ rules the earth in the Millennium. However, we are seeing a prelude to the final judgment upon the nations of the world as God avenges the righteous for the evil that has been executed upon them for the past 2,000 years.

Much of what is currently happening in the world is the result of God avenging the righteous for their suffering through the ages. Jesus said this would be one of the judgments that precede the great and terrible day of the wrath of God. **It is not the day of wrath; it is a day of vengeance.** This will be manifest in many different ways some of which we have already experienced as stated above.

THE 2012 PRESIDENTIAL ELECTION

I've witnessed ten presidential elections in my adult life. During this time I have watched the American people respond with many different reactions to the election's outcome: joy, anger, disappointment, gladness and a variety of other emotions. But the reaction to the 2012 Presidential election was unlike anything I have witnessed in my lifetime.

The celebration by one side could be compared to the day Japan surrendered at the close of WW II. The other side responded as though the world had just come to an end (and that adage is not far from reality). It was a testimony of the painful reality of how divided we have become as a nation. Differing ideologies have placed a great gulf between two people groups that can no longer coexist in a harmonious way.

For some, the following days and weeks were difficult. Serving as Senior Pastor in my church I was greatly challenged about what to share with my congregation on the Sunday following the election. As I was preparing for Sunday morning I found it difficult to set aside my personal feelings, and seemed to be losing the battle in my thoughts and meditative prayer time. After several days of wrestling within, I felt the Spirit of God remind me of Paul's prophetic words in II Thessalonians 2:10-12. Although I had studied this passage of scripture many times before, it seemed to be the message for the hour.

"Strong Delusion"

In Paul's message to the Thessalonians he is speaking prophetically about what will happen in the final days leading up to the revealing of the Anti-Christ and the return of the Lord (The Apocalyptic Age). Prophetically he said God would send, **"Strong Delusion"** and he stated the reasons why.

> [10]*"And with all deceivableness of unrighteousness in them that perish; because they received not the love of the truth, that they might be saved.*
>
> [11] *And for this cause God shall send them strong delusion, that they should believe a lie:*
>
> [12] *That they all might be damned who believed not the truth, but had pleasure in unrighteousness"*
>
> 2 Thessalonians 2:10-12

Notice the words, **"with all deceivableness of unrighteousness in them that perish, because they received not the love of the truth...".** Unrighteousness is used like a mighty weapon that equips and empowers crafty leaders to deceive those who follow them. The reason they are so successful with their deception is because their followers love not the truth. Truth is the light that exposes lies and deceit, but if one does not love the truth deception is knocking on his door.

In scripture, **"Truth"** is not just the state of being true, as the word truth can be rightfully defined; truth means more than that. In scripture truth is a person and that person is our Lord and Savior

Jesus Christ the Son of God. Jesus said in John 14:6, **"I am the way, the truth and the life…".** When the world rejects truth as revealed in scripture they also reject Christ. And the rejection of Christ is the pathway that leads to all lies and deceit.

Paul goes on to say, *"…for this cause God shall send them strong delusion, that they should believe a lie".* As I have already stated in chapter seven, there are dire consequences to those who reject the Son of God. In this prophetic revelation given to the church a strong delusion sent by God Himself is the consequence of rejecting Christ. Then Paul gives three reasons for this strong delusion:

> The reason they are so successful with their deception is because their followers love not the truth.

1. That they should believe a lie.

2. That they all might be damned.

3. Who believed not the truth, but had pleasure in unrighteousness.

In the message I shared with my church following the election I made this statement, **"The American people voted the way they did because God sent strong delusion upon them."**

The result of this election was a fulfillment of the prophetic words in II Thessalonians in two major ways: **First** a "Falling away" and **Secondly** "A Strong delusion".

A Falling Away…In II Thessalonians 2:3 Paul said, *"…for that day shall not come, except there come **a falling away first**".* Before the revealing of the Anti-Christ and the return of the Lord the prophecy teaches us that there will be a falling away of the

Church. Apostasy will sweep across the church world and many would be deceived and depart from the fundamental beliefs of true Christianity. **The 2012 Presidential election is living proof that the apostasy has already begun because it is the apostate church that voted him in.**

Several months before the election, a minister of the gospel was interviewed by a TV reporter who questioned him about the President's recent public statement giving his approval of same sex marriage. The minister was asked what he thought about his statement. The minister expressed his disapproval and disappointment of the President's position. Then the reporter asked, what will you do come Election Day? The minister responded, "I don't agree with him, but he's still the best man for the job".

In the book of Romans 1:18-32 the apostle described those who were under a judgment from God because they refused to retain God in their knowledge and worshiped and served the creature (man) instead of the creator (God). The judgment against them would have an effect upon their mind which would be manifest in their moral judgment. The word used is *"reprobate"* and has the meaning of being *"void of moral judgment"*. Because of their idolatrous sin against God and themselves, God would alter their ability to know sound moral judgment.

This altered state of mind would be evidenced by what the Bible calls *"Vile passions"*. Then the Apostle described these vile passions as women who changed the natural use of their body for that which is against nature. And men *"...leaving the natural use of the woman, burned in their lust for one another, men with men committing what is shameful"*.

When leaders, political and church leaders give their approval for same sex marriage, they have boldly announced to the entire world that they have already been judged by God and do not know the difference between right and wrong. Over 50% of American people voted for this kind of leadership. If ministers of the gospel believe this kind of leader is the best man or woman for the job that judgment has also fallen upon them!

Strong Delusion...The evidence of the *"strong delusion"* sent by God manifested itself on Tuesday November 6, 2012. I saw people mesmerized in jubilant celebration as their favorite candidate took the election by a landslide. In reality they sold their nation and their freedom to a socialist political agenda that was born during the 20th century by atheistic communism which plans to dismantle America's role as the leader of the free world.

> When leaders, political and church leaders give their approval for same sex marriage, they have boldly announced to the entire world that they have already been judged by God and do not know the difference between right and wrong.

What a masterful delusion! And it could not have happened without the help of God. There can be no other explanation. Why else would America vote for four more years of the worst Presidential term in American history? The outcome of the vote was a judgment sent from God, **"because they loved not the truth but had pleasure in unrighteousness"**. The present leadership in the White House is a judgment sent from God to avenge the righteous, not only in America but the entire world! For, as goes America...so goes the world!

Days following the election political analysts began to theorize why the Republican candidate lost. I was amused at their comments; they made reference to this statement or that policy, a poorly organized campaign, etc. What they failed to realize was that the election was lost about 40 years ago. Political decisions made in recent American history led to our present demise. I will name just a few:

1. The removal of prayer from our public schools

2. The removal of Biblical teaching from curriculum

3. The removal of God and Judeo-Christian influence in Government

More than voting for a candidate or a particular political party the people voted against the God of the Bible. They love not the truth, therefore they cast their vote!

ILLUSION, DELUSION & DISILLUSION

I will explain the outcome of the 2012 Presidential election with three words:.

1. **Illusion** – Illusion is defined as deception, a misapprehension of the true state of affairs, a figment of imagination.

Many are familiar with the world famous illusionist, David Copperfield. An illusionist is one who has the art and skill of creating an illusion in the minds of people. David Copperfield is one of the greatest. In 1983 he caused the Statue of Liberty on Liberty Island to disappear before a live audience and live television, with no camera tricks. This illusion is recorded in the Guinness Book of World Records as the largest disappearance ever performed by a magician.

Did the Statute of Liberty disappear? Of course not! However, he created the illusion that it did. Today this great Illusionist has some fierce competition, but it's not from his competitors in the world of entertainment. His competition is in Washington and wherever politicians are campaigning for the next election.

Politicians have become the great illusionists of the modern world. Making the Statute of Liberty disappear was a marvel. However, it was nothing compared to making more than half of the voting constituency of the most powerful nation on earth believe that one man has the answers to prosperity after four years of the most failed record of any presidency in American history. Now that takes a really great Illusionist!

2. **Delusion** - But the Illusionist had some help, God sent a **strong delusion**. The word delusion is taken from the root word illusion and is defined as, *a symptom or form of mental disorder, a false belief or impression upon the mind.*

Paul said, God sent strong delusion that they should believe a lie. No one with an honest sense of judgment could say, "We need four more years". No, one would have to be delusional to believe this is the path to a better America.. This is a lie and those who are delusional bought it.

When a person is delusional, they believe things exist that don't really exist. They see things that are not really there; or they may deny the existence of things that really do exist. This is what a billion dollar campaign can do to a nation of people that are suffering from a strong delusion sent from God.

How masterful they were at creating imaginary stats of supposed success. They were also skilled at diminishing the truth or making it completely disappear before live audiences and live television. If I were David Copperfield, I would be concerned about my place in the Guinness Book of World Records. And I would not suggest the other side was much better. There is a serious lack of integrity in our world, and it is on both sides of the aisle in politics.

3. **Disillusion** – This next word is what we will face in the near future. Disillusion means to be set free from the Illusion. "Dis" means to undo. It is when the lie of the illusion is exposed and you realize that the Statute of Liberty never really disappeared after all. When this happens, it will not be a pleasant experience for the American people. Take a look at what is happening in Greece. As their economy lunges forward to total and complete collapse with 25% and rising unemployment, there is rioting in the streets, anger and hostility are out of control. Nationwide anarchy threatens a governmental collapse. This is the same path America and the rest of the world have chosen.

The Apostle stated the reason why God would permit this to come upon them. *"That they all might be damned who believed not the truth, but had pleasure in unrighteousness"* II Thessalonians 2:12 KJV. This too is a testimony of the "Day of Vengeance". This is a judgment against a nation, for the blood of many cry out from the ground to the Lord God of heaven.

This is a picture of today's world...*our* world...*my* world...*your* world. Every word spoken prophetically by the Apostle 2,000 years ago has come to pass in our present time. In America, our culture has found pleasure in unrighteousness just as the prophetic word predicted. In II Timothy 3:4 scripture also says men will become *"lovers of pleasure more than lovers of God"*. This is who we are, Americans have become a narcissistic people obsessed with pleasure and it doesn't matter what level of unrighteousness we have to stoop to, as long as we have what we want.

We are faced with a very sobering question, **"Has our obsessive love of pleasure and rejection of Jesus Christ caused America to become damned by God"?** Have we... like Israel of old, one time blessed and highly favored by God, become damned because we loved not the truth and have found pleasure in unrighteousness?

America will never be the same. The days of my childhood and yours are history. There was a time when I believed we, the Church, would turn things around and make the world a better place. The problem with that kind of thinking is that it was never God's plan for man to make the world a better place. Making the world a better place

> **A**mericans have become a narcissistic people obsessed with pleasure and it doesn't matter what level of unrighteousness we have to stoop to, as long as we have what we want.

is a creative act that belongs to the Creator of the universe, not man.

WE CAN MAKE A DIFFERENCE...!

Can we make a difference? Yes! If I didn't think we could make a difference, I would never have devoted 37 years of my life to preaching the message of the cross of Christ. I would not have built my first church. I would never have crossed the oceans of the world to preach the message of Christ on foreign soil. I never would have taken on the assignment from the Lord to write this book. We can still make a difference just as others have made a difference for the past 2,000 years.

Everywhere the message of the cross of Christ has penetrated the darkness of this present world, it has produced change, miraculous change by the power of that old rugged cross. The Great Commission is still the supreme priority in the heart of God. The word "Go..." uttered by our savior 2,000 years ago is still the command to the Church of Jesus Christ today (Matthew 28:19). Go to your neighbor; go to your family; go to your friends; and go wherever the Spirit of God bids you to go…just go! And when you go, share with them the message of the Gospel of the Kingdom, for Jesus said,

> [14] *"And this gospel of the kingdom shall be preached in all the world for a witness unto all nations; and then shall the end come"*

> Matthew 24:14

There is an unresolved mystery in science, religion and every culture of the known world. That mystery is, **"when will the end come"?** Jesus answered that question in one short sentence. The answer is **"And this gospel of the kingdom shall be preached in all the world for a witness unto all nations; and then shall the end come"**.

Take the message to the nations of the world…And then shall the end come!

HOPE FOR ALL

CHAPTER 9

We understand that faith is for the now and hope reaches out into the future. In the midst of all these things there is hope. The eternal message given to us in the Word of God presents the only hope we can truly believe in. But the hope the Bible speaks of will not be found in the here and now. The Bible gives us hope in a Kingdom that is not of this present world.

When Jesus was brought before Pontius Pilate, Pilate asked Him *"...Are you King of the Jews?"* Jesus answered, *"...My Kingdom is not of this world"*. We must remember, our Kingdom is not of this world! Our hope is in that which is yet to come, not this present world.

Our hope is not new leadership in government. It is not in... "Change we can believe in". And my next statement, mainly to the church world, might challenge some of you, "Our hope is not in a revival that will change our world". That would be a great experience for most of us but it is not the hope revealed in the Bible.

We should always pray and believe for a spiritual awakening; for I believe it is the will of God to manifest Himself in a supernatural way to every generation that is born. However, it is wrong if we stop there! Our hope does not stop with a great spiritual awakening that will enlighten our world into spiritual renewal. We will take as much of that as He is willing to give us but that is not the final hope of the believer.

In I Corinthians 15:19 Paul said something about hope that we need to understand: *"If in this life only we have hope in Christ, we are of all men most miserable."* The problem with putting all our hope in revival or a move of God to straighten out our world is that revival is in *"this life"*. Paul said, if our hope is *"in this life only"* we are of all men most miserable. He didn't just say we are miserable but we are the most miserable of all people.

I have known many who have devoted all their energy and passion in trying to create an atmosphere where the great move of God can take place. Some have done it for a lifetime hoping to find the secret formula that will finally change our world. I am thankful for their passion to change our world, but after multiple decades of disappointing effort many of them have become disillusioned and "most miserable".

Proverbs 13:12 says, *"Hope deferred makes the heart sick."* Many who pursued the path of revival are living with a sick heart. They have not been able to lay hold of that which they have put their hope in. Revival seems like a logical solution to a spiritually dead sin sick world. But the problem is, revival evades us. It always seems to be just out of our reach. Try as we may we just can't seem to lay hold of it, it always seems to slip away. Perhaps God has a better plan. Could it be that His ways are not our ways?

The Word of God is a lamp to our feet and a light to our path.

In the illuminated path of scripture there is no theology for revival and we are not told to pray for revival or a move of God to fix our world. Jesus said to His disciples, pray after this manner, "Thy Kingdom come, thy will be done...".

If this present world were going to respond to a powerful, dynamic spiritual revival where miracles happen, it would have happened in the first century with the ministry of Christ and His disciples who followed Him. They performed miracles, manifestations of such that have not been repeated in 2,000 years. How did the world respond? They crucified Jesus, persecuted the miracle-working first century Church and most of the apostles, if not all, died a martyr's death. I wish I could say today's world is different, but it is not. If Jesus walked the shores of Galilee today they would crucify Him just as they did 2,000 years ago.

We preach, "This world is not our home" but we live like we want it to be. Do you know that God never intended for the world to exist forever in the state it is in at this time. God created the earth to be a temporary place for our temporary existence in this life as we know it. Scientists tell us there aren't enough natural resources for humanity to exist forever. This is true, but there will be enough to finish the mission God gave to Adam in the garden and that was to "replenish the earth" (Genesis 1:28 KJV).

Our hope is in the promise of a new world. The Bible promises there will be a New Heaven and a New Earth: for the first heaven and the first earth will pass away.

> "Now I saw a new heaven and a new earth, for the first
> heaven and the first earth had passed away..."
> Revelation 21:1

Every place where hope is mentioned in scripture it reaches out to the world that is to come, not this present world. In II Corinthians 4:18 (KJV) Paul was encouraging the church during a time of great hardship and distress when he said, *"While we look not at the things which are seen, but at the things which are not seen: for the things which are seen are temporal; but the things which are not seen are eternal"*. In this context of scripture he continues to reach out to the eternal things to give comfort and encouragement to many who were suffering great affliction.

In our present world church leaders repeatedly present the latest revelation truth that will give their followers a breakthrough from their sufferings and affliction. Yet, daily we learn that those who promise such breakthrough for their followers could not even find it for themselves. Once again, Proverb 12:13 states, **"Hope deferred makes the heart sick"**. There is no secret formula. There is no new revelation. There is something better. God is going to make all things new!

> *2 And I John saw the holy city, new Jerusalem, coming down from God out of heaven, prepared as a bride adorned for her husband.*
>
> *3 And I heard a great voice out of heaven saying, Behold, the tabernacle of God is with men, and he will dwell with them, and they shall be his people, and God himself shall be with them, and be their God.*
>
> *4 And God shall wipe away all tears from their eyes; and there shall be no more death, neither sorrow, nor crying, neither shall there be any more pain: for the former things are passed away.*
>
> *5 And he that sat upon the throne said, Behold, I make all things new. And he said unto me, Write: for these words are true and faithful.*
>
> Revelation 21:2-5 (KJV)

Use your imagination for a moment. *"God shall wipe away all tears from their eyes"*. Metaphorically or literally, it tells us that there is a day coming when God will personally take away the pain from our body and soul. There shall be no more death, neither sorrow, nor crying, neither shall there be any more pain. Think of a life where there will be no more death and sorrow, which is always followed with crying and great pain. A pain free life...the very thought is incomprehensible, for so many live with great pain and suffering. Emotional pain and physical pain many live with it every day of their lives.

> There is no secret formula. There is no new revelation. There is something better. God is going to make all things new!

This is what I imagine when I read this scripture. One day I will have a personal audience with God my Father. I believe it will be just Him and me. During that time I believe He will explain to me the things about life that I just have not been able to understand. Things about Himself and the many decisions He makes that do not make sense to me now.

I believe at that moment He will do for me what I have done with my children when they were young and innocent. Many times I sat with them, held them in my arms when they were still young enough and explained why Dad had to do this or that. Sometimes they would understand, but whether they did or not, I would wipe away their tears, give them a big hug and make sure they knew that I loved them and I would always be there for them.

It was always a special moment. Their tears would eventually dry up and a little smile would begin to emerge. Was the problem fixed? No, but before I would let them go, they knew I loved them and they knew everything would eventually be alright in life and also between me and them. Perhaps this moment with our Father will be something like that. No one really knows, but one thing is for sure, "*And He that sat upon the throne said, Behold, I make all things new*" Revelation 21:5. He promised a new life free from sickness, pain and suffering; a new heart free from sorrow; and a new world where people love one another.

Can you imagine a world where there would be no more hatred and killing? A world where sickness, disease and sorrow cannot exist. A world free of wars and death. A world where people love one another and coexist in harmony with the Omnipotent Creator of the universe. It takes quite an imagination to picture such a world. But we have something better than an imagination we have a revelation given to us in the Word of God. That revelation is the biggest picture I have in the depths of my soul. I can't see it with the natural eye but I see it in my mind, I see it in my heart, it has become just as real to me as the world in which I live.

Oh dear Friend, please open your heart to the promise of the Lord. He has a plan! Let go of all the superficial promises and meaningless hope offered by so many and lay hold of what God has said. His word can be trusted. He cannot lie. It will come to pass, and though I will probably never meet most of you who read this book in this life, one thing is sure, if you know Christ as your Savior, I will meet you some day. It may not be until we get to the other side in the new world I speak of, but one day we will have an eternity to sit down and catch up on some small talk. I hope one of those moments will be with you!

EPILOGUE

WHY SHOULD WE BELIEVE BIBLICAL PROPHECY?

PROPHETS, PROPHECIES AND ESCHATOLOGY

The studies of this book have been based upon Biblical Prophecy. A fair question would be "Why should we believe in Biblical Prophecy?" We will attempt to answer this question.

Many sources of prophecy exist in the world today. Just about every known religion in the world has within its beliefs some kind of prophecy. Islam, Buddhism, Mayans, the American Indians, all have prophecies about their past, present and future. We, as Christians, believe the only sources of prophecy that can be trusted and that has proven to be authentic are the Prophecies of the Bible. I will give you the reasons why we believe this to be true.

First, we must have a clearly defined understanding of the Prophet, Prophecy and Eschatology.

PROPHETS

It is very clear in the book of Genesis, which is the Biblical account of creation, that God created man for His Divine purposes. When God decides to do something in the earth His choice is to use man (meaning mankind) to accomplish that which He has purposed to do. He did not choose to use angels or other angelic beings such as celestial or terrestrial beings; His choice was to use man.

When God wanted to communicate a message to His people He chose a man, and called that man a Prophet. The key person in the study of this book is the Prophet. The ministry of the prophet is seen in both the Old and New Testament writings, although the role of the prophet in the New Testament changed from that of the Old Testament, the Prophet is used by God in both historical writings.

What is a Prophet? A Prophet is the person to whom God has spoken concerning present and future events. As we study the prophets in the Scriptures, all of them fulfilled a most profound role in God's interaction with His covenant people and the world throughout history. These Prophets declared the mind of God to the people from generation to generation. Prophets addressed present as well as future events; the focus of this study includes both.

In the Old Testament there were three authority figures through which God carried out His work, Prophet, Priest and King. The **King,** such as the beloved King of Israel, King David, represented government. The **Priests** were the mediators between God and the people; they managed the work of the temple and made sacrifices to God on behalf of the people. The **Prophet** was the spokesmen, the voice of God to the people.

The Voice of Man Becomes the Voice of God

The Apostle Peter gave us insight as to how God was able to use a man, in spite of his human frailty and accurately communicate his message. Peter wrote by the inspiration of the Holy Spirit *"...no prophecy of Scripture is of any private interpretation, for prophecy never came by the will of man, but holy men of God spoke as they were moved by the Holy Spirit."* (II Peter 1:20-21)

Notice the word **"moved"** in this scripture. It is used in a meta-phorical way, such as how a sailboat is driven by the wind. The sailboat is not moved by its own power, but by the wind that drives it. Peter likens this inter action between the writer and the Spirit to that of a ship and the wind.

The Apostle Paul wrote several things concerning the scriptures that help us to understand this process of God communicating His thoughts to the Prophets. In his letter to Timothy he wrote, *"All Scripture is given by inspiration of God, and is profitable for doc-trine, for reproof, for correction, for instruction in righteousness, that the man of God may be complete, thoroughly equipped for every good work."* (II Timothy 3:16-17)

"Inspiration" has the meaning of, **God breathed, or the breath of God.** In Genesis 2:7 (KJV) the scripture says *"And the Lord God formed man of the dust of the ground, and **breathed into his nostrils the breath of life;** and man became a living soul."* When Adam sinned in the garden he lost the breath of God, which led to spiritual death; resulting in separation from God and eternal dam-nation. When man receives the scriptures he not only becomes intellectually enlightened by knowledge but receives the breath of God, that which was lost when Adam sinned. As he receives the breath of God he becomes **"Born Again"** and once again be-comes alive spiritually.

The Apostle Paul further emphasized this truth when he wrote to the Thessalonians *"...because when you received the word of*

God which you heard from us, you welcomed it not as the word of men, but as it is in truth, the word of God, which also effectually works in you who believe." (I Thessalonians 2:13)

Although the Prophets were mere men, they were men chosen by God and admitted into the Divine council chambers where God *"reveals His secrets"* to men (Amos 3:7). Once God revealed His secrets to the Prophet, he was then commissioned by God to deliver the message to the people by both preaching and writing the prophetic message.

The understanding of this Biblical truth is an absolute for the reader to receive the message that has been communicated to us by God through the Prophets. Much more can be said on this subject but the reason for this writing is not to prove the inerrancy of scripture, but to bring to light the profound message that has been given to us by the Prophets about the End Times.

The Old Testament Prophets foresaw the coming of the Messiah. Jesus Christ is the main subject of Bible Prophecy and the most detailed and dramatic prophecies in the Bible are about the Messiah. They prophesied in most accurate detail about His birth, life, death, resurrection, ascension, second coming, His Kingdom and more.

Prophecy

We have already seen the fulfillment of many Biblical prophecies in the study of this book. Daily, Biblical prophecies continue to be fulfilled as the War of Gog and Magog come together right before our eyes.

To further validate the authenticity of Biblical prophecy I am going to list some of the Old Testament prophecies and its fulfillment in the times of the New Testament about the birth and life of Jesus.

- Isaiah 7:14, subject: **His Virgin birth,** fulfilled in Matthew 1:18-23. Isaiah's prophecies were given approximately 700 years before Jesus was ever born.

- Isaiah 61:1-2 subject: **His ministry in the Spirit**, Fulfilled in Luke. 4:18-21

- Isaiah 53:4-5 subject: **His Healing Ministry**, fulfilled in Matthew 8:16-17; Mark. 1:32-34; Luke. 4:40-41.

- Micah 5:2, subject: **Place of His birth**, fulfilled in Matthew 2:1-6. Micah gave this prophecy about 740 years before Christ birth.

- Zechariah 11:12-13 subject: **Betrayal for 30 pieces of silver,** fulfilled – read Matthew 27:1-10. This prophecy was given by Zechariah approximately 500 years before Christ birth.

The Old Testament included more than one hundred distinct prophecies about the Messiah. These fulfilled prophecies of Christ provide overwhelming evidence of the Divine origin of scripture and the prophetic writings that are contained in those scriptures.

When we read the prophetic writings of scripture we must embrace the same attitude about that which has been written as Paul spoke of to the Thessalonians *"...because when you received the word of God which you heard from us, you welcomed it **not as the word of men, but as it is in truth, the word of God**..."* (I Thessalonians 2:13). If you wrestle with doubt concerning the prophetic writings of the Bible, the study of this book will help remove that doubt and enable you to see for yourself that the scriptures are truly **"The Word of God."**

25% OF THE BIBLE CONTAINS PROPHECY

The study of prophecy is important; more than 25% of the Bible contains prophetic writings. Prophecy creates a word picture concerning future events and God's plan for the ages. It enables us to see. The study of prophecy can be likened to putting a puzzle together. Recently my grandson and I put together a puzzle of one of the great paintings by Thomas Kinkade. After we dumped the 500 piece puzzle onto the table we took a good look at the cover of the box, and then placed it on the table where we could make visual reference to it. This is the objective of the study of Bible prophecy. Piece by piece we assemble a picture, a picture of the near and distant future of God's covenant people and the world according to the prophetic writings of scripture.

In John's gospel, chapter 20, after Jesus resurrection he appeared to his disciples for the first time. Thomas, one of the twelve, was not present when Jesus first appeared to them. Eight days later Thomas was with the disciples and they began to tell him about Jesus' visit. Thomas, commonly known as the doubter said *"unless I see I will not believe."* As I stated before, the study of prophecy enables you to see! To doubt is to be human, but it has been said "seeing is believing." What you see, by the study of Bible Prophecy will increase your faith in God's word and has the potential to change the way you see the world and interpret what is happening prophetically at this time.

TELL ME THE FUTURE

Have you given much thought as to why we have a desire within us to know what will happen in the future? This yearning in the heart of every man, woman and child to know the future is put there by God Himself. The purpose for which God has put this longing within us is to cause us to seek God for answers, for He alone can reveal to man the secrets of what is yet to take place.

The evidence of this deep need to know the future is often seen in the movie making industry. Have you noticed how many movies come out of Hollywood about time travel? One of the most popular in our generation is the movie with Michael J. Fox "Back to the Future." They are either going back in time or going forward into the future. Part of the success of movies with this kind of theme is due to the inward desire of man to know what is going to happen in the days ahead.

> The purpose for which God has put this longing within us is to cause us to seek God for answers, for He alone can reveal to man the secrets of what is yet to take place.

Further evidence of this, "need to know" is seen in the practice of the occult. Our adversary the devil understands this. That is why he has created an imitation for every manifestation of God and that includes prophecy. Psychics, horoscopes, palm reading, tarot cards, crystal balls and the like are imitations of the devil to take advantage of the vulnerability of man in his curiosity to know the future.

FAMILIAR SPIRITS

Are these occult imitations real? Yes, some of it is real; some of it is fakery and deception. The Bible teaches us that there are familiar spirits. A familiar spirit is a demonic spirit that is familiar with you. (Lev. 20:27) They know people and study people. These spirits are able to communicate information to one who practices witchcraft and reveal secrets about one's personal life. This is an abomination of God and forbidden.

God warned Israel in the Old Testament that those who yielded their life to such a practice would bring a curse upon themselves, and to the third and fourth generation that follows them. (Exodus 20:5) This explains why those who have participated in such, or relatives in their ancestry that have practiced this, have very troubled lives. Sometimes this curse is manifested in premature deaths, sickness, poverty, divorce and many other problems that have robbed people of God's best.

We are warned by God to have nothing to do with such practices (Deuteronomy 18:9-14) and in Leviticus 20:27 God commanded Moses to put to death anyone that was a wizard or who had a familiar spirit. The command was to stone them with stones.

This is why the message of the saving grace of Jesus Christ is so important. When you receive Christ as your savior the curse of sin is broken and you become a New Creation in Christ. (II Corinthians 5:17) As a new creation, you are now blessed with all spiritual blessings in heavenly places in Christ (Ephesians 1:3), no longer subject to the curse of sin and the terrible consequences that follow. The believer is blessed, not cursed!

The Message of the Prophets

To better understand and interpret the message of the prophets we must comprehend the twofold nature of their message. Two words describe what they communicated, **(1) Forthtell (2) Foretell.** To **"forthtell"** is to address issues that were in the "now" at the time the prophecy was given to the prophet. To **"foretell"** is to speak of those things that pertained to a distant future.

Consider this example. Jeremiah prophesied to the southern kingdom, Judah, of the soon coming invasion and destruction of Jerusalem by the Babylonian empire. (Jeremiah 2:1 – 6:30) The invasion would be led by Nebuchadnezzar the king of Babylon. Jeremiah saw this prophecy fulfilled in his life time, from 605-586 BC. This is **forthtelling**.

He also prophesied of the modern day invasion of Bagdad, in Jeremiah chapters 50 and 51. We know it as the Iraqi war that began in 2003 by the U.S. and allied forces. As we studied in chapter one, modern day Bagdad is the ancient city of Babylon that is mentioned in scripture. Those prophecies are **foretelling;** we are seeing them come to pass in present time.

It is hard for us to understand but often in scripture when God addresses a nation prophetically He speaks to them about issues from the beginning to the end of their existence. God speaks from timelessness; time is relevant to man not God.

The Mercy of God

I have often heard people say "I don't like the study of Prophecy, it's a message of fear and "doom and gloom." Some may have used it for that purpose, but that is not the intended purpose for which it is given.

There is a very important truth concerning both the foretelling and forthtelling prophetic message. They testify of the mercy of God. God speaks of these things in advance to give those to whom the message is spoken an opportunity to change, such as the way God used Jonah as he prophesied to Nineveh.

Jonah prophesied to Nineveh *"Yet forty days, and Nineveh shall be overthrown."* (Jonah 3:4) Nineveh believed the word of the prophet, repented of their sin and God spared that city of judgment. God's primary desire is to have mercy, not execute His threatened punishment. This is the hope of prophecy.

Think about the nature of prophetic warnings. When a warning is given in advance it is for the hope of preservation. I have lived much of my life on the Gulf Coast of Louisiana, hurricane alley. Thank God for NOAA! Their science predicts and forecast (forthtell) tropical cyclones days in advance that we might be prepared for the imminent danger. Thank God for the warning that is given by way of science and meteorologist. Those who heed the warnings take necessary actions to protect their property and their lives.

> God speaks of these things in advance to give those to whom the message is spoken an opportunity to change, such as the way God used Jonah as he prophesied to Nineveh.

The same is true of Prophecy. Prophecy is mercy extended to our generation and that means you. All who hear the warnings, call upon the Lord, and receive Christ as their Savior will experience mercy instead of the judgment of God.

A cyclone is approaching our world that is unparalleled to anything that has happened since the creation of man. Jesus predicted it in Matthew 24:21 (KJV) after the prophecy about the signs of the times, *"For then shall be Great Tribulation, such as was not since the beginning of the world to this time, no, nor ever shall be"* (Revelation 6:1-20:3). But this cyclone will not be limited to the coastal regions of certain populations. This is a warning given to the entire world that has not come by way of science, but by the Prophetic voice of God to this generation.

How is it Possible for God to Reveal the Future?

God is not like man. We see life with everything having a beginning and an end. A child is born, becomes an adult, lives his life span and he dies. God is an eternal being; He had no beginning and He will have no end. Approximately 90 A.D. Jesus appeared to John on the Isle of Patmos and revealed to him the Apocalypse which is the Revelation of the things that will take place in the future. Jesus identified Himself to John as *"Alpha and Omega, the beginning and the end."* (Revelation 1:8) Alpha is the first letter of the Greek alphabet and Omega is the last letter. God is eternal, and from creation to consummation He is Lord of all.

Because God is "Infinite", and we are "Finite", which means we are limited and God is not, there are some things we will never fully understand until we receive our glorified bodies when the Lord returns. It is incomprehensible to man that God knows everything; He is Omniscient which means "All Knowing." He never learns anything and that includes everything that will ever take place in the future. He can reveal His secrets to the prophets because He knows in absolute detail everything about the future.

Our finite (limited) mind wants to object to such an idea that God knows everything about the future. As impossible as that may seem to mortal man let me suggest something that we are familiar with in modern times that may help with this mind bender. Have you ever considered that man, on a daily basis, is able to see into the future? This scientific human ability enables us to be who we are and accomplish the many scientific marvels of our day. Here is an example.

Target...Satellite!

In 2008 the U.S. military shot down a spy satellite orbiting the earth. The reason they shot it down while still in space was because the satellite had a 1,000 pound hydrazine tank (rocket fuel) that scientist feared would not burn up during re-entry. If the fuel tank survived it would be potentially dangerous for certain populations.

The science of successfully accomplishing such a mission is mind boggling. Consider just a few of the facts. The target satellite, the size of a school bus (which in the vastness of outer space is about comparable to a grain of sand on the sea shore) was traveling over 17,000 mph. The three stage destroyer rocket (a Raytheon SM-3) that would attempt to hit the satellite would be traveling nearly 5,000 mph approaching it in an oncoming collision course. The combined speed of both objects was over 22,000 mph. The scientist said it was like a bullet hitting a bullet on a designated spot of the bullet. Can you imagine the mathematical calculations it took for this to happen? Now of course, without computers, the calculations would be impossible.

The Perspective of a Rocket Scientist

A friend of mine and Bible teacher at the church I pastor is a retired scientist (Rocket Scientist) by the name of David Wilkens. David is a genius; he has an incredible mind. David worked with NASA on the space program with the Gemini, Apollo missions and also the Space Shuttle. I could give many accolades on behalf of David (which he would never approve of) and his many scientific achievements but the greatest thing about this man is that he is a scientist that believes in God and knows Christ as his Savior.

Knowing David's history with the space program I asked him to give a scientific, but condensed version of the science involved in shooting down this satellite. Below is David's rendition of what it took to do this.

Notice the words: Predict, Forecast, Prophesy, and also Past, Present and Future in his writing. For a layman, the wording is complex and challenging to follow, but it has its purpose, which is to illustrate a significant point in this study. Please read the following by David Wilkens:

"To appreciate what it took to shoot down this satellite you must consider the complexity of space and the different orbits in which satellites exist. First of all, satellites are placed in different types of orbits and for various reasons. Weather satellites are placed directly over the equator in an orbit plane even with the plane of the earth's equator and these orbits are circular, with the earth at the center, or focus, of the circle. Most orbits are elliptical rather than circular, for reasons of the particular mission. An ellipse does not have a single focus like a circle. It has two foci and the earth is located in one of the two foci of the ellipse. There is nothing at the other focus. Spy satellites are sometimes placed in polar orbit so the earth will turn round and round under the satellite, giving the satellite full view of the earth one section at a time during successive orbits. Other satellites have orbits inclined to the plane of the earth's equator to provide specialized views of the earth. The orbital equations are different for elliptical orbits than for circular orbits and they are much more complex.

Whatever the type of orbit a satellite might be in, intercepting it to destroy it requires a rendezvous in space similar to but different from the rendezvous that occurred every time a Space Shuttle or a Soyuz would exchange crews and truck supplies to the International Space Station. In a Space Station rendezvous the supply craft is launched to achieve the same position in the same orbit as the Space Station and then the computer will control small rocket engine pulses for closure using radar to detect and control separation and closure rates and final docking.

Achieving rendezvous requires simultaneous solution of the trajectory (in this case, both orbital) equations for both craft, a process carefully controlled to avoid collision and damage. Achieving intercept for destruction uses a different process for a different purpose—destruction. Collision is the objective. The intercepting

Raytheon SM-3 had no explosion on impact. It destroyed the errant satellite by brute force of impact.

In order to rendezvous or intercept in space, it is necessary to know (predict or forecast) where the target craft will be in some future time frame. Then the supply or destroyer craft is sent to that point at that same time. Prior to the end of the sixteenth century, mankind did not know the exact laws of motion of the planets nor had he discovered the mathematical equations that complement these planetary laws.

The German astronomer Johannes Kepler, studying under the Danish astronomer Tyco Brahe, discovered, or reasoned, that planetary orbits were ellipses and not circles. Kepler was then able to formulate three laws of planetary motion which then could be put into mathematical expression. Prior to Kepler, it was already known by some astronomers that the planets were revolving around the sun, but not knowing the laws of planetary motion or the related mathematics, it was not possible to **"predict", or "forecast", or "prophesy,"** if you will, the exact **future** position of one of the planets. Knowledge of **past** positions of the outer planets was not very helpful because in a man's single lifetime he could not observe that some of the planets circle the sun more than once. Earth circles the sun every 365.25 earth days, one earth year. Other planet periods are Mercury–88 earth days, Venus–226 earth days, Mars—1.9 earth years. Jupiter through Neptune range from 11.9 earth years to 165 earth years. Pluto's period is 248 earth years.

Kepler's discoveries allowed mankind to **"predict", or "forecast",** or if you will, **"prophesy"** the position of planets around the sun at any future (or past) time. Kepler's laws and equations are also used to describe the motion of satellites around the earth. Physically, satellites around the earth are like planets around the sun. The orbital path in each case is determined and controlled by balancing the centripetal force (gravity between the central mass and the orbiting object) with the centrifugal force of the orbiting object due to its trajectory speed.

To make the subject mission even more complicated let us consider a few more facts:

The earth spins on its axis and the surface speed of a spot on the equator is 1,000 mph. The spot will make one complete circle of 24,000 miles (the circumference of the earth at the equator) in one day or 24 hours. The ship from which the rocket was launched was moving in a forward direction and being tossed by the waves of the sea. A launched rocket always encounters some measure of crosswinds. The 1000 mph speed of the earth's equator is used to advantage and amounts to an initial boost for the spacecraft launch if it is launched toward the east. The other (by comparison minor) uncertainties in initial conditions and launch must be adjusted for with mid-course corrective guidance and engine gimbal and thrust control programs. To constantly update a spacecraft or rocket guidance information for flight control, radio signals from the craft are sent to earth computers and along with ground radar information, updates to the in-flight computer are made, similar to the way GPS satellites track signals from our cars here on earth and constantly update our travel GPS systems. The spacecraft, in its trajectory, is constantly asking the ground computer—"Where am I, where am I?" And the ground computer responds and tells the spacecraft where it is. To achieve impact in this example, **the scientists had to know in advance** exactly where the target satellite would be in order to program the guidance system on the destroyer rocket to hit the target. By way of mathematical calculations they had to be able to **"see"** into the future and illustrate on paper or computer screen, exactly where both objects would be at a given time to accomplish their goal. Then the destroyer rocket was launched on a ballistic (parabolic) trajectory and impacted the target craft in its orbital (elliptical) trajectory. The killer rocket did not have to achieve orbital speed of 17,000 mph. It only needed to follow a ballistic trajectory speed of 5000 mph to impact the target. Any launch at a speed under 17,000 mph does not achieve orbit and follows a ballistic trajectory. That's why intercontinental missiles are called "ballistic" missiles.

If man can do all of that with a finite mind, I think God who is infinite, can also **"see"** into the future and communicate to man what He sees.

In the Kingdom of God, God has given ordinary mankind abilities to discover laws and develop complementary mathematics and processes to **"see"** into the future. Paul spoke of these abilities when he said,

> [7] *"For who makes you different from anyone else? What do you have that you did not receive? And if you did receive it, why do you boast as though you did not?*
>
> 1 Corinthians 4:7 NIV

Just as God can **"see"** into the past, He has given mankind a measure of ability to do that too. For example: by running computer simulation programs to "simulate" solar system motion, one not only can forecast future lunar and solar eclipses, but by running the program backwards (using negative time in the model) one can determine when, historically, lunar and solar eclipses occurred in the past.

The occult world receives counterfeit "seer" capability from the kingdom of darkness, which is ruled by Satan. Magic, witchcraft, divination, and all other acts of sorcery are condemned in the Bible, throughout the Bible. The Bible does not deny the existence of these sorcery powers because they are real, but the Bible does condemn them because they are wicked and evil.

Mankind also **"sees"** into the future when he **"forecasts"** or **"predicts"** revenues, expenses, and profits for a business or other enterprise. By keeping and reviewing records, he will **"look into the past"** for results to guide him in his predictions or forecasts for the **future."**

David Wilkens
Scientist, Space Program

Now we understand that prophecy is not a compilation of mathematical equations; it is a manifestation of the Spirit of God. We only use these thoughts in an analogous way to illustrate a great mystery and manifestation of the Spirit of God. Jesus used analogies and metaphors repeatedly in His ministry. You must know this, neither I nor a scientist like David would pretend to fully understand everything about the Omniscience of God because we, like you, have a finite or limited minds. As the scripture previously stated (I Corinthians 4:7), God has shared some of His attributes with His creation. They are called communicable attributes of God. Every ability man has come from his creator and that includes every scientific achievement of our age.

A Metaphor
A Wheel in the Middle of a Wheel

I want to share with you a metaphor that has helped me over the years to try and comprehend this marvel of our creator. In Ezekiel 1:16 we have the Biblical account of Ezekiel's vision of the work of God in the earth; he described it as **"a wheel in the middle of a wheel."** I want you to think of the mechanical way in which a wagon wheel works, it is very simple. The wagon wheel has a hub in the middle of the wheel which spins on an axle that is stationary, the axle does not move. Out from that hub are spokes that extend to the outer rim of the wheel.

Here is the metaphor, the axle which does not move represents where God sits in timelessness. Everything subject to time is constantly moving; notice the second hand on your watch. Where God sits in timelessness, (the axle which does not move) He can look out to the outer rim of the wheel and see all at once different dispensations of time, which are constantly moving, just as the spokes reach out from the hub to the outer rim. The spokes can represent different dispensations of time. God sees everything from beginning to end all at the same time.

I see this in the book of Revelation. In the fourth chapter of Revelation Jesus said to John " *"Come up here, and I will show you things which must take place after this"* (Revelation 4:1b). John had an "out of body experience" as he was taken up into heaven and sat where God sits in timelessness. He told John to write the things he sees. What John wrote is that which he could see from God's eternal perspective. In chapter 12 of the book of Revelation we have a prophetic picture of this metaphor of the wheel in the middle of the wheel. I will explain.

Remember the axle in the metaphor which does not move, this is where God sits in timelessness. Just as spokes reaching out from the hub to the outer rim, John could see different dispensations of time. John described a woman being with child travailing in birth. This represented the Nation of Israel from which the Messiah, Jesus was born. Remember, John could see this which took place approximately 90 years before he saw it and wrote about what he saw, he could see the past. He also wrote "There appeared a wonder in heaven...a great red dragon... and his tail drew the third part of the stars of heaven, and did cast them to the earth."

This represents the fall of Lucifer and one third of the angels of heaven that rebelled with him when he tried to overthrow the throne of God. (Ezekiel 28, Isaiah 14) This took place at least 4000 years before the time of John's writings, but he could see it, once again he could see the past. Then, in verse 5 you can see the ascension of Jesus after His resurrection which was once again the past, for John was in the present. He could also see His rule in the millennial reign which will not take place until Jesus comes back to earth, and this event will take place in the future. John could see all these past, present and future events all at the same time. Now if that doesn't give you a mental hernia you're just numb!

Thoughts like these greatly challenge us, but this is what prophecy is all about. God who can see everything at the same time, allows His prophets to enter His secret chamber, see a small portion of what He sees and commission them to write it down and preach it to the nations of the world. He is **"a wheel in the middle of a wheel."**

ESCHATOLOGY

The particular aspect of Bible Prophecy we have studied in this book is Eschatology. Eschatology is the area of systematic theology that focuses on the last things, whereas, "Prophecy" is a broad term that embraces all prophecies from the Book of Genesis to Revelation. Eschatology focuses on the last prophecies to be fulfilled. The term is derived from a combination of Greek words, *eschatos,* meaning "last", and *logos,* meaning "word." The English suffix *logy* denotes "doctrine, study, or science of." Thus, we have the word "Eschatology"... the doctrine of last words.

I am amazed at how little attention is given to the prophetic writings of the "Last Words" (or Eschatology) by our contemporary writers, pastors and Biblical teachers. We are living in the age of the fulfillment of the "last words". Because we are, it is our due diligence to give our undivided attention to those prophecies that have been written about our time.

JESUS IS COMING BACK

One basic truth about Eschatology that almost all evangelical theologians agree upon is that Jesus is coming back. Christians base their hope on this prophetic promise. It is called the **"blessed hope"** in Titus 2:13 the scripture says, *"looking for the blessed hope and glorious appearing of our great God and Savior Jesus Christ"*. The Greek words makaria elpida (blessed hope), might be better translated the "joyous anticipation." Those who know of His return anxiously and joyously await this great event.

APPENDIX

THE BLOOD RED MOON OF PROPHECY

The cover of Pastor Mark's book on end-time prophecy has a blood red moon on it. The Lord told the prophet Joel, "*I will show wonders in the heavens and on the earth, blood and fire and billows of smoke. The sun will be turned to darkness and the moon to blood before the coming of the great and dreadful day of the Lord*" (Joel 2:30-31 NIV). Peter quoted this passage from Joel Chapter 2 in Acts Chapter 2 on the day of Pentecost.

Fire and billows of smoke can make the moon appear red, especially at moonrise and moonset when the light reflected by the moon has to travel through many more miles of air to reach the observer. Oxygen and contamination (like smoke, smog or dust) in the air scatters the short-waved blue-region light leaving the longer wave red-region light to reach the observer. That is why our sky looks blue, because oxygen scatters blue light. Oxygen itself is not blue. Observers on earth have reported sighting a dark red moon when there are forest fires or volcanoes. And rarely the moon has appeared dark red just from blowing dust.

The most significant blood red moon ever recorded in history was caused from the explosion of Krakatoa, a volcano in the Indonesian archipelago; the moon appeared blood red for over a month.

Blood moons can also occur during lunar eclipses. A lunar eclipse occurs when the moon enters the earth's shadow on the opposite side of the earth from the sun. The center cone of the earth's shadow is very dark and is called the umbra. Outside the umbra is a region of less dark shadow called the penumbra. A total eclipse of the moon (a completely dark red moon) requires the moon to move fully into the umbra, the very dark part of the earth's shadow. If the moon moves partially into the umbra and partially into the penumbra, it is called a partial eclipse. If the moon moves only into the penumbra and not into the umbra at all, it is referred to as a penumbral eclipse and the moonlight will only be diminished by a small amount.

Total eclipses of the moon cause the moon to look red because the earth's shadow will block direct sunlight on the moon. But, the earth's atmosphere acts like an optical lens and refracts (bends) light passing through the atmosphere and "projects" it on the moon. Since this sunlight has travelled through a lengthy distance of earth's atmosphere, the blue-region light is scattered and filtered and only the red-region light reaches the moon and reflects back to earth.

The blood red moon in the referenced passage from Joel will occur before the coming of the day of the Lord and we can and should watch for it. Prophecy watchers are excited by the Lunar Eclipses Chart on NASA's website which shows four consecutive total lunar eclipses, which is called a "Tetrad". Another Tetrad will occur from April, 2014 through September, 2015(April 15, 2014; October 8, 2014; April 4, 2015; and September 28, 2015). What is of interest to students of Bible Prophecy is that this Tetrad will fall on Jewish Feast days or New Years Days.

The last two times there were Tetrads were in 1949-1950, just after the Nation of Israel was rebirthed and in 1967-1968, about the time when Israel recaptured Jerusalem from the Muslims. These previous Tetrads and their relationships to events in Israel lead to great anticipation about what prophetic event (like maybe the rapture) might occur coincident to the next tetrad in 2014-2015. There will not be another Tetrad in this century.

The day of the Lord is quite clearly a reference to the Tribulation. In the prophetic sense it does not speak of a 24-hour day but a season of time. In our time (or we could say "in our day"), it is common to use expressions like, "in the day of Lincoln" that would refer to the time Lincoln lived—not a specific day but a season, a period of time—with duration maybe specified and maybe unspecified. All biblical descriptions of the day of the Lord given by prophets like Joel (Chapter 2), Amos (Chapter 5), and Zechariah (Chapters 12 & 13) match the description of the Tribulation (or Jacob's trouble) given by Jesus (Matthew Chapter 24), Jeremiah (Chapter 30), Daniel (Chapter 12), and John (Revelation Chapters 6-20).

It is necessary and wise to distinguish between the "Day of the Lord" and what the Bible refers to as "The Day of Christ". The day of the Lord is always referred to as a time of great judgment, persecution and suffering. The day of Christ is identified in I Corinthians 1:7-9, 5:5; Philippians 1:10, 2:16 and II Thessalonians 2:2. The day of Christ is always described as a hopeful and joyful event that we should eagerly await.

Compare the description of the day of the Lord in Joel 2:30-31 with what Paul says of the day of Christ in I Corinthians 1:7-9 (NIV). Paul says, *"Therefore you do not lack any spiritual gift as you eagerly wait for our Lord Jesus Christ to be revealed. He will also keep you strong to the end, so that you will be blameless on the day of our Lord Jesus Christ. God, who has called you into fellowship with his Son, Jesus Christ our Lord, is faithful"*. The "Day of Christ is the rapture". The "Day of the Lord" is the Tribulation.

When John was taken up into heaven he saw a blood-red moon (and the sun was black), not before the Tribulation but well into it. This happened as Jesus opened the sixth seal on the seven sealed scroll. Revelation 6:12-17 (NIV) says, *"I watched as he opened the sixth seal. There was a great earthquake. The sun turned black like sackcloth made of goat hair, the whole moon turned blood red, and the stars in the sky fell to earth, as figs drop from a fig tree when shaken by a strong wind. The heavens receded like a scroll being rolled up, and every mountain and island was removed from its place. Then the kings of the earth, the princes, the generals, the rich, the mighty, and everyone else, both slave and free, hid in caves and among the rocks of the mountains. They called to the mountains and the rocks, 'Fall on us and hide us from the face of him who sits on the throne and from the wrath of the Lamb! For the great day of their wrath has come, and who can withstand it?' "*

We have discussed things in natural law that cause a blood red moon. But, God's power does not require Him to use natural law to cause signs in the heavens, although He might choose to. God can overrule natural law (which He also created) and speak anything He wants into existence. He may use natural processes and the laws of physics to cause a blood red moon or He may just speak it and it will happen.

A couple more important facts, NASA says there will also be a ring of fire solar eclipse April 29, 2014 and a total solar eclipse March 20, 2015, adding further excitement to the anticipation about what these "signs in the heavens" might introduce during this amazing season. A total eclipse of the sun occurs when the moon comes between the earth and the sun and completely blocks the sun. The sun will be black, like what John the Apostle saw when God let him see the future in Revelation Chapter 6. A black sun solar eclipse will only occur if the earth is far from the sun in its elliptical orbit around the sun. If the earth is near the sun in its elliptical orbit, the sun appears too big and the moon cannot completely block the sun. That phenomenon is called an "annular" or "ring of fire" eclipse.

Just so anticipation does not lead to unbridled speculation, it should be recalled that God told Joel that the blood moon before the day of the Lord would be accompanied by blood and fire and billows of smoke. That scene does not rule out a lunar eclipse but it does not require one. It could result from a volcano or war.

One thing is certain; the Blood Red Moon is a sign of the Apocalypse. If the prediction by NASA of a Blood Red Moon does not reference the much feared and anticipated Apocalypse revealed in scripture, it is a fearful reminder of that which is to come.

David Wilkens
Scientist, Space Program